METEOR
FROM THE
COCKPIT

METEOR FROM THE COCKPIT

METEOR
FROM THE
COCKPIT

Peter Caygill

Pen & Sword
AVIATION

623.7464
CAY

First published in Great Britain in 2010 by
PEN & SWORD AVIATION
An imprint of
Pen & Sword Books Ltd
47 Church Street
Barnsley
South Yorkshire
S70 2AS

ISBN 978 1 84884 219 9

Printed and bound in England
By the MPG Books Group

Pen & Sword Books Ltd incorporates the Imprints of Pen & Sword Aviation, Pen & Sword Family History, Pen & Sword Maritime, Pen & Sword Military, Wharncliffe Local History, Pen & Sword Select, Pen & Sword Military Classics, Leo Cooper, Remember When, Seaforth Publishing and Frontline Publishing

For a complete list of Pen & Sword titles please contact
PEN & SWORD BOOKS LIMITED
47 Church Street, Barnsley, South Yorkshire, S70 2AS, England
E-mail: enquiries@pen-and-sword.co.uk

Website: www.pen-and-sword.co.uk

Contents

Acknowledgements		01
Introduction		02
Chapter 1	Design and Development	03
Chapter 2	Into Action	08
Chapter 3	Flying the Meteor III	16
Chapter 4	Testing the Meteor IV	23
Chapter 5	Trials with the Meteor F.8	30
Chapter 6	The Meteor F.8 Described	37
Chapter 7	Meteors over Korea	41
Chapter 8	Flying Tiger	47
Chapter 9	Structural Failures	55
Chapter 10	The Meteor Night-Fighter	68
Chapter 11	Accidents and Incidents	75
Chapter 12	Meteor QFI	100
Chapter 13	Spinning the Meteor	109
Chapter 14	Pilot Debrief (1)	115
Chapter 15	Pilot Debrief (2)	130
Appendix	Meteor Structural Failures, 1946–53	139
Glossary		142
Index		145

Acknowledgements

Much of the research for this book was carried out at the National Archives at Kew, and I should like to thank the staff for their courtesy and assistance during numerous visits.

This book could not have been written without the enthusiastic support of former RAF pilots who flew the Gloster Meteor, and I am deeply indebted to them. In alphabetical order they are as follows: Geoff Amor, Dennis Barry, Alan Colman, Malcolm de Garis, F. Eastman, Trevor Egginton, Graham Elliott, Howard Fitzer, Bob Hillard, Paul Hodgson, Barry Holmes, Derek Morter, Ted Nieass, Peter Sawyer, Bruce Spurr, Peter Vangucci and Ian Wilson.

In particular I should like to thank Alan Colman for sharing his experiences of flying the Meteor with 74 'Tiger' Squadron at Horsham St Faith, and later as an instructor at No. 211 Advanced Flying School at Worksop. As well as describing in detail what it was like to fly a Meteor and some of the hazards that had to be faced, his accounts give a fascinating insight into life on an RAF fighter squadron in the early 1950s.

Finally, I should like to thank Philip Jarrett once again for supplying many of the photographs that are reproduced in this book.

Introduction

I first came across the Meteor in the late 1950s as a young aircraft enthusiast living near RAF Leeming in North Yorkshire. At that time Leeming was home to the Javelins of 228 OCU, the unit tasked with training crews for the RAF's all-weather fighter squadrons, but a number of Meteors had been retained as hacks and for target-towing duties over the North Sea. Although the Javelin was an impressive machine, not least for the glorious noise made by its Armstrong Siddeley Sapphire engines, the Meteor also fired the imagination of a six-year-old boy. Its shape may have been less than inspiring compared to the swept-wing fighters entering service, but it was still capable of a fair turn of speed at low level, and the 'blue note', that particular characteristic of the age, was frequently heard as pilots indulged in a little throttle bending.

The Meteor will be forever remembered as the first British jet fighter to enter squadron service and the only jet-powered Allied fighter to see action in the Second World War. Subsequent development was limited as a result of its relatively conventional airframe, but with its powerful Rolls-Royce Derwent 8 engines, a well-flown F.8 was quite capable of causing an upset if a Sabre pilot attempted to mix it in mock combat below 20,000 ft. The Meteor was also immensely strong, and many pilots owe their lives to its rugged construction. A story that did the rounds in the 1950s told of how a pilot attempting a single-engine landing opened up to full power on the good engine only for his aircraft to perform a complete barrel roll on short finals, before crashing into the undershoot area and finishing in a crumpled heap at the end of the runway, having demolished most of the approach lighting on its way. Despite such an unorthodox arrival, the pilot walked away unscathed.

For a whole generation of pilots the Meteor (or the Meatbox, as it was affectionately known) provided the ideal introduction to the realms of jet-powered flight. Despite the fact that it introduced a new technology to the skies, it was utterly dependable, and engine failures were few and far between. The Meteor did suffer a high accident rate, but many of the losses were due to a lack of knowledge of the stresses imposed by high-speed flight at low level, and a misguided training programme that killed many pilots during simulated single-engine landings, a real-life eventuality that very rarely occurred. Although it was no thoroughbred, the Meteor inspired great affection from its pilots, many of whom felt a degree of sadness when it was time for them to move on to more advanced aircraft. Incredibly, more than sixty years after its first flight the Meteor lives on, as it is still used by Martin Baker to test the company's ejection seats – testimony, if that were needed, of the basic soundness of the Meteor design.

CHAPTER 1

Design and Development

Although the design of what was to become the Meteor was first seen in a preliminary brochure submitted by George Carter, chief designer of the Gloster Company, to the Air Ministry in August 1940, the aircraft's roots can be traced back to the first attempts to perfect a gas turbine engine for use in an aeroplane. The relative simplicity of this type of engine was, perhaps, its major attraction, given the increasing complexity of high-powered piston engines. Early work in Britain in the field of gas turbine technology centred on experiments by A.A. Griffith and H. Constant at Farnborough in the 1920s with axial-flow engines driving a conventional propeller. This type of compressor was capable of greater efficiencies than a centrifugal compressor, but although the theory was simple enough, the temperatures and pressures generated were too much for the metals available at the time. This lack of success unfortunately had a detrimental effect on work being carried out by another pioneer, Frank Whittle.

Whittle had encapsulated his ideas in a thesis while still a cadet at RAF Cranwell in 1926, and following spells as a fighter pilot with 111 Squadron at Hornchurch, as an instructor at 2 FTS at Digby and as a test pilot at the Marine Aircraft Experimental Establishment at Felixstowe, he was dispatched to Cambridge University to take a degree in Mechanical Engineering. While at Cambridge he designed his first jet engine, and after the formation of his own company, Power Jets Ltd, this was run for the first time on 12 April 1937. With a lack of official interest and limited financial backing, progress was painfully slow, but following the start of the Second World War the Air Ministry began to look on Whittle's work more favourably, to the extent that it placed an order for a jet engine to power an experimental aircraft.

Of the British manufacturers, only Gloster had sufficient capacity to take on the design, and it was more than happy to do so as George Carter had already met Frank Whittle and knew of his work. The Air Ministry issued Specification E.28/39 to cover the project, and Carter, in close collaboration with Whittle, began his design of what was to be the first British jet-powered aircraft. The somewhat corpulent result was of all-metal monocoque construction with a low-set wing and tricycle undercarriage. Initially consideration was given to mounting the tail unit on a twin-boom layout with a short jet-pipe to minimise thrust losses, but concerns over possible airflow breakdown over the tail led to this being discarded in favour of a more conventional design, with the jet-pipe exhausting aft of the elevators and forward-set fin and rudder.

The E.28/39 (W4041) was initially fitted with a W.1X engine of 750 lb.s.t. for taxi trials that were carried out by P.E.G. Sayer, Gloster's chief test pilot, commencing on 7 April 1941. Even though the engine was not cleared for flight, Sayer made several short hops from the grass airfield at Hucclecote. After the completion of these tests, W4041 was dismantled and taken by road to Cranwell, which was more suited to the first flight of such an important aircraft, in terms of both facilities and security. With the flight-approved W.1 engine of 860 lb.s.t. installed, Sayer made the first flight in W4041 on 15 May 1941, and the aircraft was to go on to have a highly successful career before it was finally retired and put on permanent display in the Science Museum in London.

Although the E.28/39 was primarily a vehicle to test a new form of propulsion, consideration was given to a more practical use as an interceptor fighter with an armament of four 0.303 in. Browning machine-guns. The very low thrust levels of the early jet engines, however, meant that, for the time being at least, a single-engined jet fighter was out of the question and the only practical choice was to go for a twin-engined design. Even before the little E.28/39 began to take shape, George Carter was forming his ideas on just such a machine that could be developed into an operational jet fighter. His eventual proposal, which formed the basis of Specification F.9/40, was of mainly conventional design with twin jet engines mounted on low, straight wings. What was new, however, was the use of a tricycle undercarriage and high-set tail to keep the horizontal surfaces well clear of the jet efflux. The wing-mounted engines allowed the main spar to be taken right across the centre section, which provided great strength, while at the same time saving weight. The fuselage was relatively slim in section, and the initial proposal of carrying six 20 mm Hispano cannon in the nose was soon reduced to four to avoid excessive weight on what was still likely to be an underpowered machine.

In early February 1941 production of the F.9/40 prototype was given the go-ahead, and an order for twelve 'Gloster Whittle' aeroplanes was placed in the serial range DG202–DG213. In the event, the number of prototypes was reduced to six before being increased to eight, the last prototype to fly being DG209. For a time the F.9/40 was referred to as the Rampage, and later as the Thunderbolt, but to avoid confusion with the American Republic P-47 fighter, the name Meteor was eventually chosen. As there was little that could be termed radical in the Meteor airframe, its progress was relatively straightforward, which was in marked contrast to the development of the Whittle engines. Serious difficulties were experienced with compressor surge, which limited power, and a lack of production drawings from Power Jets induced the engine's manufacturer, the Rover car company, to come up with its own solutions to numerous other problems, much to Whittle's annoyance. The working relationship between Whittle and Rover went from bad to worse, to the extent that by late 1942 hardly any progress was being made at all, and prototype Meteors were piling up at the Gloster company awaiting flight-cleared engines.

In the meantime another centrifugal jet engine had been developed by Frank Halford at de Havilland, which employed a single-sided impeller with air only entering at the front, instead of the double-sided impeller used by Whittle. Due to the problems with the Whittle engine, the fifth prototype (DG206), powered by Halford's H.1, was the first to take to the air on 5 March 1943 at Cranwell, with Michael Daunt at the controls. This flight took place a full eight months after the first taxi trials of DG202 with Whittle W.2B engines. The impasse between Power Jets and Rover was eventually broken by the intervention of Ernest W. (later Lord) Hives of Rolls-Royce, who suggested to Rover that it swap jet engine production for Rolls' tank engine factory at Nottingham. The arrangement suited both parties, and with the weight of Rolls-Royce behind it, Whittle's jet engine programme moved forward with increased impetus, so that DG205 flew for the first time on 12 June 1943 with W.2B engines. DG202 finally made it into the air on 24 July 1943 to join the growing engine test programme.

July 1943 also saw the completion of DG204, which was radically different from any of the other F.9/40 prototypes. It was powered by two Metrovick F2 axial-flow turbines, which were carried in underslung nacelles and were far more advanced than the centrifugal jet engines designed by Whittle and Halford. Although they had the potential of delivering high thrust levels, they were much more complex and were also heavier. DG204 began taxi trials on 4 August, but was beset by the excessively high idling thrust of its F2 engines, which had to be removed and returned to Metropolitan-Vickers for modifications. DG204 was flown for the first time on 13 November 1943 at Farnborough, but was lost in a crash on 1 April 1944 when the aircraft broke up in the air following disintegration of one of the Metrovick engines during a high-speed run at 20,000 ft. Although the pilot, Sqn Ldr Douglas Davie, managed to vacate his aircraft, he died later from the injuries that he sustained.

During early test flying of the Meteor, one of its less desirable characteristics soon became apparent – that of directional instability, or snaking. Various remedies were put forward, most of which involved either a reduction or an addition to the area of the aircraft's vertical tail surfaces. At first it was thought that the lack of a destabilising effect as a result of the aircraft not having propellers might be the cause. Surmising that the fin and rudder might have been made too large, some aircraft had the ventral fin and tail bumper removed, and one even flew with the fin and rudder above the horizontal tail surfaces removed. It was all to no avail, however, as the snaking persisted.

The flight test schedule was joined by DG203, which was first flown on 9 November 1943, powered by W.2/500 engines of 1,640 lb.s.t. Before take-off on its second flight, the compressor of one engine exploded, causing a large amount of damage to the nacelle and centre section, but luckily Michael Daunt was able to walk away unscathed. At this early stage in development, engine failures were an ever-present hazard, and Daunt had already experienced a rear bearing failure in flight in DG205, from which he made a successful single-engine landing. Engine surge was another phenomenon that was experienced on a regular basis, as evidenced by a series of violent pops or bangs from within the engine as the flow became irregular. Many different modifications were put in place but the problem took a long time to sort out.

In the meantime the remaining Meteor prototypes had taken to the air, and the development programme moved forward at ever-increasing pace. Tragedy struck again on 27 April 1944 when John Crosby-Warren was killed when DG205 crashed at Minchinhampton Common, near Stroud in Gloucestershire. Following stability and fuel-consumption tests in the morning, Crosby-Warren had been required to carry out a series of high-speed dives, during which his aircraft suffered a failure of its aileron tab, which created severe aileron flutter, leading to loss of control. At the time of the accident DG205 was testing a new spring tab design that would ultimately be used on the Meteor F.8.

The loss of DG205 was offset by the reappearance of DG203 after repair, but after a few short flights it experienced another impeller disintegration when being flown by Michael Daunt at 5,000 ft. Once again, most of the debris disappeared through the top of the cowling, but with damage to the nacelle and tailplane, the aircraft had become dangerously unstable in roll. Daunt jettisoned his canopy but elected to stay with his aircraft and try to save it. In spite of very limited control he was able to make a successful landing in a potato field, quipping afterwards that the 'Whittle-Daunt potato-lifter chipper cooker' had worked well!

The loss of two Meteor prototypes with a third on long-term repair did not delay the testing programme, as the first production Meteor Is were beginning to appear, powered by W.2B/23 Welland engines. It was at this time that Wg Cdr H.J. 'Willie' Wilson was recalled from a posting to the USA to command a new unit attached to the RAE at Farnborough to begin the conversion of the first batch of service pilots to the Meteor. Wilson's flight quickly gained jet experience with the

E.28/39 and the American Bell XP-59 Airacomet that had been on test in the UK since September 1943, in exchange for the first Meteor I (EE210), which was transported to Muroc Air Force Base in California in February 1944. By June 1944 the first Meteor Is were delivered to the RAF in the shape of EE216, EE217 and EE218, and these were joined by EE219 on 1 July.

The last prototype (DG209) was taken on its first flight on 18 April 1944 and was the first Meteor with the more powerful W.2B/37 engine, rated at 2,000 lb.s.t. This became the Derwent I as fitted to the Meteor III. The remaining prototypes continued in the development programme until the end of the war, their individual histories being as follows:

Aircraft	First Flight	Engine Type	Remarks
DG202	24/7/43	W.2B/23	Used for flight trials at Newmarket, Moreton Valence and Rolls-Royce, Hucknall.
DG203	9/11/43	W.2/500	Became trials aircraft for W.2/700. Became instructional airframe 5926M.
DG204	13/11/43	Metrovick F2	Engine trials at RAE Farnborough; crashed 1/4/44.
DG205	12/6/43	W.2B/23	Used by Gloster and de Havilland, Hatfield; crashed 27/4/44.
DG206	5/3/43	Halford H.1	Trials by RAE – also by Gloster and National Gas Turbine Establishment.
DG207	24/7/45	Halford H.1b	Sole prototype F.II, used by de Havilland Engine company for trials.
DG208	20/1/44	W.2B/23	Aerodynamic trials with Gloster, later used by de Havilland.
DG209	18/4/44	W.2B/37	Engine trials with Rolls-Royce, Hucknall, scrapped Farnborough July 1946.

CHAPTER 2

Into Action

With the transfer of jet engine development from Rover to Rolls-Royce, the supply of engines capable of delivering sufficient thrust for flight at last began to catch up with the number of airframes produced by Gloster, and in April 1944 it was announced that 616 (South Yorkshire) Squadron would be the first operational unit to fly the aircraft. Dennis Barry was a flight commander at the time, and recalls his conversion to the Meteor:

'Right then, chaps, part of the squadron is to be re-equipped with a new type of aircraft. Two flights will retain the Spitfire VIIs, but the third flight will re-equip – with Gloster Meteors.' The speaker was Sqn Ldr L.W. Watts DFC, the Commanding Officer of 616 Squadron, and the setting West Malling aerodrome. The date was April 1944, and the news that 616 Squadron was to become the first Allied unit to operate jet aircraft was very welcome; we were extremely excited and felt privileged to be chosen to operate this unique type of aircraft. We moved to Fairwood Common, near Swansea, where a couple of Oxfords were delivered. These were intended to help us to convert from our single-engined Spitfires to twin-engined aircraft, to learn asymmetric flying and to give a landing aspect. We were familiar with the usual three-point landings with our Spitfires – stick back, hold the aircraft off then a gentle stall into a three-pointer – but now we had to become used to landing nose forward, as if the aircraft had a tricycle undercarriage. We then moved to Culmhead to keep operational while we converted to Meteors, flying long-range sorties over the Channel.

On D-Day, 6 June 1944, I flew with four other 616 Squadron pilots in the Oxford to Farnborough to attend the CRD conversion unit. We were converted in groups of five and ours was the second course. Wg Cdr H.J. 'Willie' Wilson, a test pilot, was in charge and he welcomed us with details of the background development of the new aircraft and its Welland engines, all in a top secret atmosphere. On the following day we were briefed for our first flights. We clustered around the Meteor, peering into the cockpit while the wing commander went through the cockpit drill, explaining the instruments and its flying characteristics. Next we were told that we could take off on our first familiarisation flights. The briefing seemed rather sparse, especially as there were few Meteors available, and so any written off would have been disastrous. There were no Pilot's Notes available, but we felt confident, if a little over-awed at the prospect of flying such a novel aircraft.

As I taxied out to the end of the Farnborough runway in Meteor I EE214/G, I ran through the drill as briefed and then positioned the aircraft ready for take-off. After holding maximum power on the brakes for a short while, I released the brakes and the aircraft accelerated slowly down the runway. There was no swing and I held the control column level until 80 mph indicated, then eased the stick back and lifted off the runway at 120 mph. With wheels and flaps up, the rate of climb was poor, around 500 ft/min, but as the power built up, the rate increased. The aircraft was quiet, with no noise from the engines, only a 'whooshing' sound from the air passing the cockpit, rather like a glider, and the visibility was good.

The Meteor felt heavy on the controls compared with the Spitfire, especially when full of fuel. Aerobatics were forbidden in the Mark I due to it being underpowered. After a forty-five-minute flight it was time for landing, remembering that one had to land straight off with no overshooting as the power dropped off when the airspeed was reduced. On landing the Meteor decelerated slowly, being rather heavy. Later, when I carried out single-engine flying, I discovered the Meteor flew well on one as there was no drag from a feathered propeller on the shut-down engine. Formation flying proved easy, but care had to be taken as any formation changes had to be done slowly as the engines took time to build up the required power. Climbing to altitude was slow, but I once reached 35,000 ft. Overall, compared to the Spitfire VII, the Meteor was easier to fly, without propeller controls, it was quieter and it had better visibility. However, it was heavier to handle due to it being underpowered, and also more concentration had to be fixed on the instruments.

Ian Wilson was another member of 616 Squadron, and got his first taste of jet-powered flight a few days after Dennis Barry:

When I was attached to RAE (14–17 June 1944) to fly the Meteor, Wg Cdr Wilson took one look at my flying-logbook and told me that he had flown more aircraft types than I had flying hours, which was only a slight exaggeration! Later, he visited us frequently while we were at RAF Manston. He arrived in his Dragon Rapide along with his secretary. On several occasions he joined us in our Meteors practising formation flying. I can still recall his voice coming over the R/T saying, 'Icy calm, chaps, icy calm', whenever things got a bit rough: for instance, the time an official photographer was on board our Airspeed Oxford aircraft to photograph the formation and the pilot misjudged his approach and flew right through the middle of our supposedly tight formation. He subsequently lost out to Andy McDowall as CO of 616 Squadron. He had no combat experience, whereas McDowall had previously served with 602 Squadron during the Battle of Britain.

The Meteor was my first experience of an aircraft with twin engines (apart from a few hours on the Airspeed Oxford). Acceleration after take-off and from low-speed flight was poor compared to piston-engined aircraft, coupled with slower throttle movement, requiring much greater anticipation of the necessity to increase power. This applied particularly to the B23 Welland-engined Mark I and early Mark III aircraft. I recall that a few aircraft were fitted with a small-diameter tailpipe. This gave a marginal improvement, but too rapid opening of the throttles caused the engine to 'pop back' (I think the airflow through the engine actually reversed!).

Handling at normal to high speeds gave no problems. The aircraft was well behaved and pleasant to fly. Response to controls was good, although increased speed called for greater effort. Early aircraft were fitted with fabric- covered control surfaces, and these did prove a problem later when we carried out mock attacks on formations of USAAF Fortresses and Liberators (November 1944). We arrived back at base with very little fabric left on the rudder. I found the excellent forward vision a bit disconcerting on landing, compared to the almost complete lack of vision from a Spitfire cockpit. This occurred particularly when the nosewheel oleo was a bit soft and the aircraft was in a nose-down attitude on the runway after landing. This happened on my first Meteor flight, causing me to temporarily release the brakes. This, together with the brakes being rather ineffective, caused me to run onto the grass at the end of the runway, fortunately being brought to a halt by sinking into very soft ground.

By the end of July 1944 sufficient Meteors had been delivered to equip 'A' Flight. 'B' Flight was to retain its Spitfire HF.VIIs a little longer and put them to good use by flying reconnaissance missions over northern France to ascertain vertical and horizontal visibility for medium bomber raids on V-1 launching sites. The Meteors went into action for the first time on 27 July, flying several 'anti-Diver' patrols on the lookout for V-1 flying bombs. Sqn Ldr L.W. Watts experienced trouble with his guns as he was about to open fire on a V-1 and Flg Off T.D. 'Dixie' Dean had to break away from another when he got too close to the balloon barrage. The first success was not long in coming, however, as on 4 August Dean opened the Meteor's account when he used his wingtip to turn a V-1 onto its back, causing it to dive into the ground south on Tonbridge. Dean had been forced to adopt this tactic after suffering another cannon stoppage, which was a regular occurrence at the time, as Dennis Barry recalls:

> Trouble was experienced with the cannon, of which we had four in the nose. The linkage chutes had to be modified as the used links often became fast in the jettison chute, leading to a build-up of links in the guns and jamming the mechanism; this became a familiar problem to us. Our Meteors had not gone through Boscombe Down for testing, but straight into squadron service due to the urgency. As a result we had many visits from representatives and 'boffins' from armaments, radio, Rolls-Royce and Gloster.

By the end of August the majority of the V-1 launching sites in the Pas de Calais had been overrun by the Allied ground forces, by which time 616 Squadron's tally of V-1s stood at thirteen. For the rest of the year the Meteors were kept well away from the action over the Channel and had to make do mainly with bomber affiliation exercises and recognition sorties to acquaint anti-aircraft gunners with the new aircraft. Practice ground attack sorties were also undertaken, firing into the mudflats along the Thames estuary. Due to the clean lines of the Meteor I and lack of propeller drag, the relatively steep 'Spitfire-type' approach had to be quickly abandoned as speed built up rapidly. As the Meteor I did not have airbrakes, a much shallower approach had to be made, but this too caused problems, as there was a distinct danger of being hit by debris thrown up into the air.

An early modification that had to be fitted to the Meteor's gun-firing circuits came about as a result of tragedy, as the late Mike Cooper recalled in his book *Meteor Age*:

> Flying Officer McKenzie was taxying towards the dispersal after completing a Diver patrol. A strong wind was catching the large rudder, elevators and ailerons, swishing them back and forth and up and down, which in turn made the control column in the cockpit tend to thrash about. The gun firing button of a Meteor was on the control column and covered by a safety flap which had to be flipped back before the button could be depressed to fire the guns. This flap must have caught in the cockpit straps or the parachute harness round McKenzie's rather large stomach. Then, possibly in an effort to hold the column still, Mac pulled it firmly against his stomach, the firing button was depressed and the guns fired. The shells

crashed into a parked Meteor, killing one ground crew, injuring a company civilian representative and, of course, damaging the aircraft. To overcome this problem a micro-switch was fitted into the undercarriage circuit to prevent the cannons firing with the wheels down. We tested each aircraft over the mud-flats to ensure that the cannons stopped firing when the wheels were lowered.

The strict operating limitations imposed on the Meteors were relaxed a little in early 1945 when a detachment of four aircraft flew to Melsbroek in Belgium on 4 February, the rest of the squadron remaining at Colerne, where it had taken up residence on 17 January. The squadron had also, by now, received the first examples of the Meteor III. Dennis Barry once again:

In December 1944 we converted to Meteor IIIs and there was a marked difference between the Mark I and the Mark III. We found the Meteor I underpowered, it had an aerobatic restriction, a top speed of only 385 mph, a 'car door' type of hood and was generally rather basic with wires hanging around in the cockpit. The Mark III was more powerful, thus it had a higher ceiling, better acceleration and a much higher top speed of 495 mph. It was fully aerobatic, too, had an ordinary sliding hood, plus increased fuel capacity. The Meteor I had been powered by two Rolls-Royce Welland I jet engines, with 1,700 lb of thrust, which was not powerful enough for our purposes. The Meteor III, however, used the new Rolls-Royce Derwent engines, giving 2,000 lb of thrust.

While the rest of the squadron moved to Colerne, my flight of four aircraft flew across the Channel to be attached to the 2nd Tactical Air Force, based at B.58 Brussels/Melsbroek. This was the first transfer abroad by the squadron, and after we arrived our aircraft were painted white and flew over Allied lines at appointed times so that our troops could become accustomed to the sight of Meteors and therefore not fire on them in mistake for Me 262s. There was no opportunity for combat, as an official order restricted our flying to Allied areas, to prevent the Germans shooting one down, thus gaining the secrets of the aircraft and its engines. The remainder of the squadron joined us and we moved to Gilze-Rijen, in Holland, then to Nijmegen (B.91) airfield in support of the advancing Army. From here we flew our first operational sorties around Amsterdam and Utrecht, attacking trucks and convoys. Flg Off Mike Cooper was the first to attack, and the speed of his dive completely fooled the Germans, whose fire was well out.

By April 1945 the Meteors were operating out of B.109 Quackenbruck on German soil, and could range widely over German territory, again attacking road and rail targets and transport, once also strafing a Junkers Ju 88 on an aerodrome. We moved again to B.152 (Fassberg), and here the squadron suffered its first 'jet' casualties. However, it was an accident that caused the loss, rather than German action, of Sqn Ldr Watts and Flt Sgt B. Cartmel, who collided in cloud. [Flt Sgt Donald Gregg had been killed in a landing accident on 15 August 1944.] The same day the squadron destroyed thirteen German vehicles and damaged at least twenty-five more (a record), which helped soften the blow. In the final days of the war we destroyed many more vehicles and forced down a Fieseler Storch, which was then strafed. However, we did not have the chance to fight the enemy in the air, as we would have liked the opportunity.

Ian Wilson was another member of the initial detachment that had made history as the first Allied jets to operate from the Continent:

I joined the detachment at Melsbroek on 9 February. We shared the airfield with Spitfire PR aircraft, whose pilots delighted in making mock attacks just as we became airborne! Although photographs of the Meteor had been distributed to ack-ack units, they were classified as 'Secret' and appeared not to have reached the troops. Some of the fire we received was not very friendly, but nobody was hit. I flew back to Andrews Field on 4 March with three other pilots in an Airspeed Oxford. It was here that I recall carrying out several landings with the absolute minimum of fuel. Airborne time was severely restricted by the high fuel consumption, particularly at low altitude, and on one occasion an engine stopped on final approach due to lack of fuel following formation-flying practice over the North Sea. I also had two of my three engine failures at Andrews Field on 16 and 17 March 1945.

Back on operations, I was returning to Gilze-Rijen on 3 April when I was diverted to Eindhoven because of a thunderstorm over the airfield. After a forty-minute flight I didn't have much fuel left and aviation kerosene was not available. When the weather cleared I decided to return to Gilze-Rijen since I had just about enough fuel remaining to return to Eindhoven if necessary. I briefed a member of the ground crew on start-up procedures, removal of the starter trolley, etc., and then climbed in and started the engines. When I looked round for this airman, he wasn't there any more! Not being used to the deafening scream of jet engines at close quarters he took flight and ran off. I had no choice but to unstrap, climb down (avoiding the air intakes) unplug the lead from the starter socket, secure the cover and remove the wheel chocks. Otherwise the return flight was uneventful.

On 18 April my aircraft was damaged on take-off. So far as I was concerned everything was normal, but after I retracted the wheels the aircraft settled back onto the runway again, sliding along on the two engine nacelles. The runway was quite short and the pine woods at the far end looked awfully close. I had no means of stopping (no brakes) so just left the throttles wide open and became airborne again. Total flying time was five minutes. I still don't know why this happened. The temporary runway was PSP (pierced steel planking) laid on bare earth and the day was hot. Jet engines develop maximum thrust under cold conditions, and the take-off run can be increased by up to fifty per cent under extreme conditions, even at sea level. That runway must have been awfully hot, but even so my number two made a normal take-off formating on me – to start off with, anyway!

My third and last engine failure occurred on 24 April. My flying-logbook records 'Meteor III YQ-C, Recce Nordholz airfield, fifty-five minutes', and my comments at the time, 'Port engine hit by debris, hole in port wing, starboard engine u/s [unserviceable], fired at two fuel tankers, flak accurate.' On the return flight I switched off the starboard engine because the rear bearing temperature was off the clock. Sometime later the port engine started to overheat and sounded rough, so I restarted the starboard engine again and switched off the port one. After landing it was discovered that the oil tank for the port engine was holed and empty. Fortunately the starboard engine had kept going for rest of the flight.

Although later Rolls-Royce centrifugal jet engines developed a reputation for rugged reliability, in the early days there were a number of failures, as Mike Cooper explains:

Serviceability of the Meteor Is and IIIs posed quite a problem. Besides the gun failures on the Is, a frequent occurrence on both marks was overheating of the main thrust bearing in the engines. Pilots were told to watch carefully the jet-pipe temperature, and if the readings rose above a certain level, the engine had to be shut down. Many pilots experienced this problem, and returning to base on one engine was common. The bearings were made of plain white metal – only by substituting roller bearings for the white metal ones was the problem eventually solved.

Geoff Amor was another 616 Squadron pilot to experience engine failure. He recalls this and some other aspects of flying the early Meteors:

Shortly after flying to Melsbroek as part of the reinforcement for the detachment of four white Meteors, I had an engine catch fire on take-off due to failure of the magnesium alloy. My logbook comments afterwards were, 'Landed safely, put out fire!' The original positioning of the relight buttons was on the right hand side of the instrument panel, and I well recall the contortions one had to go through to attempt a relight. One hand had to be on the button, the other on the high-pressure cock, with the stick held between the knees. Later the relight buttons were wired onto the high-pressure cocks, leaving one hand free to fly the aircraft. We also had some fun with the drop tanks. The original 100-gallon ventral tank was a fixture and the fuel was turned on by pulling out the lever positioned on the instrument panel. When this tank was replaced by the 180-gallon drop tank (ventral) the same lever was retained, but to turn the fuel on you had to rotate the lever through ninety degrees. To jettison the tank, you pulled the lever out. There was more than one drop tank dropped at the take-off point during the change-over period, with some very red faces as a result.

Having pioneered jet-powered flight in the RAF, 616 Squadron did not survive for very long after the end of the war, as it was disbanded on 31 August 1945 and renumbered as 263 Squadron. However, it was re-formed at Finningley on 31 July 1946, flying Mosquito NF.30s, and later flew single-seat Meteors once again before being disbanded for good on 15 February 1957, along with all the other squadrons of the Royal Auxiliary Air Force.

CHAPTER 3

Flying the Meteor III

The Meteor I was quickly replaced by the Meteor III, which featured a strengthened airframe, more internal fuel (330 gallons), airbrakes, a sliding hood and, apart from the first fifteen aircraft, more powerful W2B/37 Derwent I engines producing 2,000 lb.s.t. EE249, one of the early Derwent-powered machines, was used for brief handling trials at A&AEE Boscombe Down in February/March 1945.

During trials of a Meteor I a number of criticisms had been made of the cockpit layout, and in several respects no improvement had been made. The independent adjustment of the rudder pedals was not liked, and with the rudder pedals in the fully aft position, full rudder movement was not obtainable owing to the pilot's foot fouling a cover over the control cables. As on the Mark I, the oil-pressure gauges were mounted in the centre instrument panel below the blind-flying panel and were obstructed by the control column. Oil-temperature gauges were mounted on the extreme right of the instrument panel, where they were at an oblique angle to the pilot and where the lighting was poor.

The socket for the R/T lead was still mounted on the front of the pilot's seat where it was liable to cause the lead to jam the control column universal joint, as had occurred on Meteor I EE212. The upright seating position remained the same, and with the low-set rudder pedals, it was felt that the pilot was affected more by 'g' and was liable to black out at a lower value than in other fighter aircraft. Two booster buttons were situated forward of the engine starter buttons for the purpose of facilitating engine restarting in the air. These were not incorporated on the Mark I or the Mark IIIs with Welland engines. One difference on the Mark III was that the footsteps used for access to the cockpit retracted when the undercarriage was raised instead of when the hood was closed as on the Mark I.

General handling was similar to the Meteor I, although the increased all-up weight of the aircraft was noticeable when taxiing over soft ground. Due to the increased thrust from the Derwent I at idling rpm (5,000), the aircraft would start to move on smooth tarmac when the brakes were released. There was no appreciable difference in the take-off characteristics compared to the Mark I, except that lift-off occurred at 115 mph IAS instead of 105 mph IAS, again as a result of the increase in weight. The higher thrust of the engines resulted in a shorter take-off and quicker acceleration to the initial climbing speed. A yaw to the left was immediately noticed on the initial climb, and it was necessary to use two divisions of right rudder trim at 200 mph IAS. Subsequently this setting was used for take-off. Neutral elevator trim was used instead of the 1½ divisions nose-down trim that had been required for the Mark I.

Longitudinal stability was tested at various CG loadings. At an aft CG the aircraft showed the degree of longitudinal stability at low speeds to be slightly less than that of the Mark I, the effect being felt most in turns, trimmed flight in the climb and at low cruising speeds. At a forward CG the Meteor III was very stable over the whole speed range, so much so that stick forces for manoeuvring were heavier than normal for a fighter. In between these two extremes at a typical service loading, longitudinal stability was considered satisfactory despite some deterioration at speeds below 250 mph at maximum rpm (16,400). Even so there was no tendency to tighten in turns, and the rate of divergence when disturbed from a trimmed speed was slow and not noticeable in ordinary 'hands-on' flight.

At all CG positions tested, the change of trim with power was in the correct sense, i.e. on opening the throttle the change of trim was nose up. The only exception to this was at an aft CG when there was a tendency for the change of longitudinal trim with decrease in speed at low speeds to be nose up. This had also been encountered on the Meteor I. The elevator force required to check any large change of power was moderately heavy, this being particularly noticeable when throttling back in a dive at high speed (this was a characteristic of all Meteors at all CG positions)

mph IAS	200	250	300	350	400	450
Elevator pull force – lb	8	7	8	9	10	22

On one occasion when the aircraft was in a dive the inner glass sandwich of the front windscreen blew in. It was therefore removed, but when subsequently descending from flights at altitude, both the front and side panels tended to mist up completely. There was also no method of heating the cockpit, which was extremely cold at altitude.

During turns the aileron and elevator forces were excessively heavy, but otherwise the handling characteristics were satisfactory. With CG at the aft limit the elevator forces were less, becoming very light in turns above 2 g at 320 mph IAS, and at 3 g the aircraft tended to remain in the turn on its own. A light pull force was required to produce 2 g at 320 mph IAS, but at higher speeds the pull force needed to initiate a turn was greater. At a typical service loading, elevator forces in turns at trimmed speeds between 180 and 450 mph varied from being light but responsive to moderate. There was no tendency to tighten in turns automatically.

Dives were also carried out from 12,000 ft. In trimmed dives only small movements of the trimmer were required as it was very effective at high speeds. There was sufficient forward trim over the speed range, the maximum used being one division nose down. At forward CG the pull force to recover at 480 mph IAS at about 3 g was heavy, becoming moderate at aft CG. In out-of-trim dives from trimmed level flight at 360 mph at full throttle, it was necessary to trim out the push force at 420 mph IAS, with further retrimming as the speed increased. At 450 mph IAS at 6,000 ft, the ailerons appeared to lighten off and to be overbalanced over small movements. Lightening of the ailerons was also encountered at high altitude on the Meteor I. A directional oscillation was noted during dives in bumpy air, the amplitude increasing slightly with speed. It was also discovered that if a directional oscillation was deliberately induced at 25,000 ft where the atmosphere was usually smooth, the damping characteristics were worse than at low altitudes, in that the yawing tending to continue longer. These oscillations were comparable to those of the Meteor I with a similar empennage.

Stalling speeds were a little higher than those of the Meteor I due to the increased weight. The behaviour at the stall was similar to the earlier mark, though there was a tendency to drop the right wing rather than the left. Recovery was normal.

The Meteor III was also tested by the Central Fighter Establishment (CFE) at West Raynham, which conducted a trial using EE281, EE428 and EE446. The opportunity was also taken to compare the Meteor III with one of the ultimate piston-engined fighters, the Tempest V. Flight limitations for the Meteor at the time were a maximum permissible speed of 500 mph IAS, imposed for structural considerations, which was the deciding factor at low level. There was also a Mach number limit of 0.74 at altitude. Undercarriage and flaps were not to be lowered above 155 mph IAS, and aerobatics were prohibited at weights in excess of 12,300 lb. Maximum landing weight was 12,000 lb. Intentional spinning was not permitted.

For take-off, unlike their counterparts at Boscombe Down, CFE pilots recommended that both elevator and rudder trim tabs should be set to neutral prior to running-up the engines to maximum rpm against the brakes (16,500+/-100 rpm) to check that full power was available, that jet-pipe temperature was within limits and that burner pressure was normal. When the brakes were released the aircraft accelerated fairly slowly, but using one-third flap and in conditions of zero wind it still became airborne in about 650 yards at approximately 105 mph IAS.

Once airborne, the Meteor III was pleasant to fly in calm weather. Due to the characteristics of the early jet engines, initial acceleration could at best be described as moderate, and climb performance was poor until climbing speed was reached. The best rate of climb was obtained at comparatively high airspeed and small angle of climb. For pilots used to having to contend with torque and slipstream effects of propeller-driven fighters, the Meteor's almost complete lack of change of trim on a typical fighter sortie was a major bonus. Its directional instability, especially when flying in turbulent conditions, was less welcome, and could only be cured by throttling back and reducing speed, as use of rudder tended to make the condition worse. The view forwards and to the sides was excellent but was severely restricted to the rear by the metal armour plate behind the pilot's head.

The Meteor III was capable of performing all normal aerobatic manoeuvres and would have been considered excellent had it not been for the ailerons, which were excessively heavy. As regards formation flying, piston-engine pilots had difficulty at first due to the poor acceleration and deceleration of the aircraft, and the normal fault was one of over-correction, but this was soon overcome. Formation work became easier above 300 mph IAS due to the increased power of the engines at higher throttle settings. For a formation take-off it was recommended that the leader should use 16,000 rpm, thus allowing 400 rpm for the rest of the section to use for correction, and once in the air a setting of 15,000 rpm allowed sufficient reserve for station keeping. Formation landings were straightforward, always assuming that the leader gave clear indication when he wanted undercarriage and flaps to be lowered.

Of the three controls the elevators were the lightest and were very effective. Trimmers were also provided for the rudder and elevators, which were particularly effective above 300 mph IAS and provided adequate trim throughout the speed range. There was no change of trim at 'unstick' or when the undercarriage was retracted, and a slight tendency to sink when the flaps were raised could easily be held by elevator. The rudder was heavy but effective, although this was of little use, particularly if directional snaking commenced as efforts to control this tendency with rudder only tended to make matters worse. Aileron response was good, but the amount of force required to produce any particular movement was much heavier than on any other fighter tested by CFE.

Flight at high Mach numbers produced some interesting results. At Mach 0.68 a severe snaking set in, together with lateral oscillations, although the controls at this stage were still effective. By the time that Mach 0.72 was reached the snaking had become much more violent and the stick was almost solid. On the positive side, however, a nose-up tendency was noted at this Mach number. At Mach 0.73 violent juddering was experienced, consisting of up-and-down vibrations that were transmitted to the stick, which was entirely ineffective and solid. On throttling back the controls became effective once again after a short pause. Although compressibility effects were evident at a disappointingly low Mach number, there was ample warning for the pilot, and it was recommended that the engines be throttled back at the first sign that shock waves were beginning to form. It was also found that excessive use of 'g' during recovery tended to aggravate the effects and was liable to bring on juddering at lower Mach numbers. There were also marked differences in individual aircraft, some machines exhibiting the adverse effects of compressibility as much as 30 mph sooner than others due to dirty aerofoil sections, dents in cowlings, etc.

The Meteor's high-altitude performance was also relatively poor in that the height at which the rate of climb fell below 1,000 ft/min was only 31,000 ft. At these heights care had to be taken that burner pressure did not fall below 10 lb/sq.in., but the chief concern for the pilot was the possibility of engine surge. This could occur during steady flight at altitude, and could only be stopped by gradually reducing the throttle setting, which prevented the early Meteors from achieving their calculated performance at height. Engine surge could also occur at lower levels if the throttles were opened too quickly, leading to lower levels of acceleration and irregular thrust. This could result in a yawing motion if just one engine surged, which could be extremely dangerous during certain phases of flight and especially during an overshoot. When flying in bad weather, low-level turbulence could lead to the needle of the turn indicator deflecting, so that a mean position had to be judged. In rain, visibility through the front windscreen and side panels was poor.

The Meteor III was easy to land although with flaps down the glide angle was rather shallow and speed decreased very slowly when airbrakes were not used. A normal gliding approach was recommended, with the base leg flown at 140 mph IAS and the final approach at 115 mph IAS. Pilots were advised to touch down approximately twenty yards up the runway so as to keep the angle of approach correct and obviate any tendency to undershoot. If an undershoot was about to occur the throttles had to be opened early to extend the glide owing to the poor acceleration characteristics of early turbine engines at low speed. A flat approach was definitely not recommended, as this tended to place the aircraft in such an attitude as to produce a nose-up and tail-down landing, which could damage the rear fuselage. Successful landings were made in crosswinds of up to thirty miles per hour at ninety degrees to the runway heading.

During comparative trials with a Tempest V, the Meteor III demonstrated a clear superiority in terms of top speed. This varied slightly with height as follows:

Height	Meteor	Tempest	Difference
1,000 ft	465 mph	381 mph	84 mph
15,000 ft	471 mph	416 mph	55 mph
30,000 ft	465 mph	390 mph	75 mph

Although the Tempest possessed an initial advantage in accelerations from 190 mph IAS due to the slow pick-up of the Meteor's Derwent engines, after approximately thirty seconds, and with the speed approaching 300 mph IAS, the Meteor was beginning to draw away quite rapidly, and it was out of range (600 yards) after ninety seconds. The Meteor was also superior at decelerating if its airbrakes were deployed; indeed, these were so effective that they had to be retracted once again after moving behind the Tempest to avoid dropping out of range.

Zoom climbs were attempted with a pull-out from a dive at 500 mph IAS into a forty-degree climb. Initially there was little difference between the two aircraft until the nose of the Meteor came up to the horizon, when it started to pull away rapidly. By the time it had reached its best climbing speed (225 mph) the Meteor was approximately 750 ft above and 600 yards ahead of the Tempest. It was also found that by increasing the angle of zoom, the Meteor could gain even more of a height advantage. These tests were carried out at various heights with the same results. During dives with the throttles closed there was nothing to choose between the Meteor and the Tempest. With throttles open, however, the Meteor was 500 yards ahead by the time that its limiting speed of 500 mph IAS was reached in a dive from 12,000 ft.

Due to its lower wing loading, the Meteor was also superior at turning circles and could turn inside the Tempest under all conditions and get on its tail in four turns. However, this was offset as the Meteor was at a disadvantage in initiating manoeuvres, since the Tempest could out-roll it easily at all speeds. A well-flown Tempest could thus be an extremely difficult target for a Meteor if its pilot used frequent turn reversals.

Despite the fact that the Meteor was superior in nearly all respects, the outcome of any dogfight was far from certain. Although the Tempest had no performance advantage, its crisp handling characteristics, especially in the rolling plane, were in marked contrast to the Meteor's heavy ailerons and gave it plenty of opportunity to keep the jet-powered machine at bay. The Meteor also suffered from directional snaking at higher speeds, so even if it was able to get in a firing position its pilot might find that he was unable to bring his guns to bear. CFE went so far as to state that the Meteor as tested was 'unsuitable as a gun platform at operational speeds'. To this could be added the ever-present danger of engine surge at altitude. One aspect of the Meteor that was praised was the effectiveness of its airbrakes. These were found to be extremely useful tactically, as they could be used to avoid overshooting, or to induce an opponent to overshoot into a position where the Meteor could open fire.

A total of 210 Meteor IIIs were produced, and the mark went on to serve with fifteen RAF fighter squadrons. The last fifteen production aircraft (EE479–EE493) were fitted with long-chord engine nacelles that raised the Meteor's critical Mach number to a slightly more respectable 0.76 (these nacelles were also a feature of the Meteor F.4, which was eventually cleared up to 0.78 IMN). Among the many trials that were carried out, the Meteor III was unique in that EE337 and EE387 were used for deck landings aboard HMS *Implacable* in 1950. Both aircraft were fitted with Derwent V engines in short nacelles and featured a Sea Hornet V-frame arrester-hook installed in the rear fuselage, together with a strengthened undercarriage. The trials ran to thirty-two landings and were highly successful.

CHAPTER 4

Testing the Meteor F.4

Following the success of the RAF's High Speed Flight in raising the World Speed Record to 606 mph in 1945 and 616 mph in 1946, the Meteor F.4 went on the serve with thirty-one regular and auxiliary squadrons, total production for the RAF amounting to 489 by Gloster and forty-five by Armstrong Whitworth, although seven of this batch were subsequently diverted to the Egyptian Air Force. The final F.4 (VZ436) was delivered from Armstrong Whitworth's Baginton works on 27 April 1950. Testing of the new variant was carried out by A&AEE and CFE, the latter unit producing its initial report following a tactical trial on the F.4 between December 1947 and April 1948.

The findings of the report were generally complimentary, the increased power of the Derwent V producing brisk acceleration on take-off. The F.4 could be flown off at 110 kts IAS, but if sufficient runway was available it was advisable to allow the speed to increase to 120 kts IAS before pulling back on the stick. There was no tendency to swing, and once airborne the aircraft quickly reached its climbing speed. The average take-off run was a mere 800 yards. Landing was also straightforward, and it was possible for sections of aircraft to land as rapidly as piston-engined fighters provided that the long, low, powered approach was not used. Owing to the slow response of the engines, pilots had to accustom themselves to the glide approach with the engines throttled back, although it was recommended that rpm be maintained at 7,500 or above. Speed on final approach had to be accurate as any excess speed was difficult to lose and the aircraft tended to float. The correct technique after touch-down was to keep the nosewheel off the runway to provide aerodynamic braking. Overshooting presented no difficulties provided that the throttles were opened evenly and smoothly and no attempt was made to climb until the safety speed of 145 kts IAS was reached. The minimum amount of fuel needed for one overshoot was thirty gallons.

The F.4 was considered to have excellent single-engine performance, and most aerobatic manoeuvres could be executed with little difficulty with one engine shut down. As speed decreased, more opposite rudder had to be applied to keep the aircraft straight until at approximately 180 kts IAS full opposite rudder and trim was insufficient to maintain a straight course at full power. When this occurred the good engine had to be slowly throttled back to maintain control. On one engine the final approach had to be made at the slightly higher speed of 110–115 kts IAS, and the live engine had not to be cut until it was certain that there was no risk of undershooting. Overshooting on one engine was straightforward provided that the decision to go around was made before speed had been reduced below 145 kts IAS. An overshoot below this speed was more difficult but could be carried out from as low as 110 kts IAS provided that the live engine was opened up carefully and the yaw counteracted by powerful use of rudder. The pilot also had to bear in mind that if the starboard engine had failed he would most likely have to operate the undercarriage and flaps by the cockpit hand pump, as the aircraft's hydraulic pump worked from the starboard engine.

Although the rate of climb was greater than any previous fighter aircraft tested at CFE, the climbing angle was no steeper, due to the Meteor's higher forward speed. From the cockpit the climbing attitude appeared to be very shallow, and there was a tendency for pilots to climb the aircraft too steeply unless a constant check was made on the air speed indicator (ASI). Without airbrakes the aircraft accelerated rapidly in a dive and the maximum permissible Mach number of 0.76 (at the time of test) was soon reached and exceeded. Warning of excessive speed was given by a gentle snaking motion, which was the cue for the throttles to be brought back and the aircraft eased out of the dive. With airbrakes selected the Meteor could be dived very steeply, with rapid height loss. The airbrakes were very effective at all speeds but could not be extended fully above 350 kts IAS.

The Meteor F.4 was pleasant to fly for aerobatics and could easily be rolled up to speeds of 400 kts IAS. Above this speed, however, the ailerons became progressively heavier, so that by 510 kts IAS they were practically immovable. For looping manoeuvres the elevators were light throughout the speed range and care had to be taken in the first and last quarters of the loop or excessive 'g' could well result. Use of the elevator trim tab was advisable throughout the complete loop as changes of speed were great. If a loop was commenced at 5,000 ft and 380 kts IAS, approximately 7,000 ft would be gained and the speed at the top would be in the region of 180 kts IAS. The height lost in the pull-out tended to be slightly greater than that gained in the climb, and the speed at the bottom of the loop, with throttles closed and airbrakes in, was generally around 420 kts IAS.

For operational purposes it was considered that the full loop in the Meteor was of little value and strain could easily be placed on the aircraft in the final quarter through pilots attempting to pull out of the dive too quickly. The roll off the top, however, was a useful method of utilising the exceptionally good zoom qualities of the aircraft, and was simple in execution. The Meteor was also pleasant to handle in inverted flight. At low speeds (280–300 kts IAS) the pilot had to apply a forward movement of the control column to maintain level flight, but despite this no difficulty was experienced in climbing inverted.

The Meteor F.4's stalling characteristics were straightforward, and ample warning was given when the aircraft was approaching a stall. A wing tended to drop, but this could be counteracted by coarse use of aileron, which led to the aircraft stalling straight with heavy buffeting. The normal recovery procedure of easing the control column forward and allowing speed to build up was immediately effective.

In addition to endowing the next generation of fighter aircraft with a significant speed advantage, the dawning of the jet era meant that it was possible to fly and fight at much greater heights, since the performance of gas turbine engines did not deteriorate as height was gained, as was the case with piston-engined fighters. To discover the problems that would have to be overcome if a target was to be successfully intercepted at high speed and high altitude, CFE carried out a series of trials using a Meteor F.4 from November 1947 to May 1948. The work examined the radius of turn of the Meteor F.4 at 40,000 ft, the basic problems of interception under visual conditions at these altitudes, a preliminary investigation of the problem of aiming, visual range at 40,000 ft, the effect of height displacement on visual range and the time to intercept, the effect of evasive action on the time to intercept at 35,000 ft and the meteorological conditions experienced at high altitude. The rules of interception were that evasion by the 'bomber' (another Meteor) was unlimited in azimuth but limited to a height gain or loss of 5,000 ft. After evading, the bomber had to proceed in the general direction of the objective, and it was also limited to Mach 0.74 and 13,600 rpm (the Meteor fighter was allowed to fly up to Mach 0.80 with a throttle setting of 14,100 rpm, which equated to maximum climb revs).

Many of the sorties carried out during the trial provided data as regards the Meteor's larger turning radius at 40,000 ft (compared to that at lower levels). At this height a Meteor F.4 took just over one minute to turn through 360 degrees in a 2 g turn at Mach 0.75, and this resulted in a radius of 1¾ miles. Assuming a collision course approach, it was calculated that the fighter had to turn in behind the target at 3.6 times the turn radius (6¼ miles) for a successful interception to be made. In this type of attack pilots had great difficulty assessing the target's range and also its relative course, but even when they did get it right the time taken to overhaul the target was excessive. There was a greater chance of success when carrying out collision course attacks at 35,000 ft, as the Meteor's radius of turn at this height was 1¼ miles, so that the initial turn onto the target had to be made at only 4½ miles range.

Further trials at 40,000 ft showed that the best type of attack was a crossing visual contact (non-collision course), one in which the target passed about 1½–2½ miles ahead of the fighter with a course difference of ninety degrees. With this type of approach the distance between the fighter and the target was reduced and the turn-in was made at around two to three miles range. As a result the time taken to overtake the target was reduced by about two minutes. There was one significant drawback to this type of interception, however, as radar controllers on the ground had to work much harder to direct the fighter into the correct position to commence its attack. Although the average radar detection range was in the order of fifty miles, there were a number of occasions when 'fading' was experienced, indicating a weakness in the high-level cover of the GCI station used. (RAF Langtoft in Lincolnshire). It was concluded that, wherever possible, collision-course attacks would be made up to 35,000 ft, with crossing-type attacks above this height.

With an engine speed of 14,100 rpm, the rate of climb of the Meteor F.4 fell off rapidly above 35,000 ft, and by 40,000 ft it was down to 750 ft/min, giving an absolute ceiling of around 43,000 ft. The Meteor could do better if climbed at full power (14,550 rpm), but this meant operating the engines beyond their limits. The best indicated climbing-speed was found to be 280 knots at sea level, reducing by two knots per 1,000 ft up to 20,000 ft and three knots thereafter. The average time from wheels rolling to 40,000 ft was 14½ minutes, but to achieve this the pilot had to give very careful consideration to his instruments. On reaching the operating height, a further 1.7 minutes was needed to accelerate to cruising speed. To allow for variations in engine performance and differences in handling, more time had to be added, so that the total time taken from wheels rolling to achieving cruise speed at 40,000 ft was 17.3 minutes. If full power was used throughout, this time could be reduced by four minutes. Times to height could also be adversely affected by the height of the stratosphere, which during the course of the trial varied by as much as 10,000 ft and 20°C over ICAN standard conditions.

Further difficulties were experienced during the trial, as it was discovered that at 40,000 ft, and with a target range of 1,000 yards, attacks could not be made at more than twenty degrees angle off due to the Meteor's poor rate of turn, which meant that the pilot was unable to track the target in his gunsight. Astern attacks at or near the Meteor's critical Mach number also caused problems as the target's slipstream induced compressibility effects, which usually resulted in so much height being lost as to completely nullify the attack. This applied to attacks above Mach 0.77 with an overtake speed of around 35 knots. At slower speeds compressibility effects on entering the slipstream were not as violent, and although the attack was disturbed it could be rescued quickly from outside the slipstream providing that the closing speed was not excessive.

Successful interceptions were made at heights up to 20,000 ft by approaching the target from 300 ft above. In this situation the attack could be held to close range, allowing a relatively long burst (10–15 seconds) without hitting the slipstream. This method could not be employed at high altitude, as in order to maintain a given line of flight the Meteor had to be flown at greater angle of incidence. In order to hold the target in the sight, the nose had to be lowered, and this resulted in a build-up in speed, together with a rapid loss of height, which brought the attacker into the slipstream before a long burst could be fired. Pilots also had difficulty in flying accurately, as a small alteration of incidence caused a disproportionately high rate of climb or descent.

Condensation trails depended on the atmospheric conditions and tended to occur on one day in three. Maximum visual range without contrails was shortest at 7 nm (longest 12 nm), with contrails the shortest sighting was at 8½ nm (the longest, 30 nm). It was also discovered that prolonged operations at high altitude tended to worsen the Meteor's serviceability rate, with an increased number of snags being reported as regards the aircraft's pressurisation, hydraulics and instruments.

Between June 1949 and February 1950 a standard early production F.4 (RA397) was tested at Boscombe Down to ascertain the aircraft's characteristics when flying at high Mach number. Although the Meteor F.4's service limitation had risen to 0.78 IMN, it was felt that this figure was likely to be exceeded during combat manoeuvring at high altitude and that service pilots should be made aware of the expected behaviour and the correct recovery techniques. For part of the trial RA397 was fitted with a ventral tank, but Mod.560, which introduced more powerful jacks so that the airbrakes could be opened fully at high IAS, was not fitted.

For the tests the aircraft was trimmed in level flight using 14,400–14,500 rpm at heights from 41,000 to 43,000 ft, and then pushed into dives to attain the maximum possible Mach number as quickly as possible. Continuous records of airspeed and height were taken by an automatic observer and the characteristics encountered were also noted. A running commentary was broadcast by the pilot during the dive, the initial angle of which was fifteen to thirty degrees. The characteristics noted were as follows:

0.78–0.79 IMN	Slight but rapid fore-and-aft control column movement promoting moderate porpoising. Aircraft nosing up with increasing IMN. Slight buffeting.
0.80 IMN	Change of longitudinal trim to nose down, but forces of small magnitude.
0.81 IMN	Porpoising and buffeting. Tendency to drop port wing. Wing could be raised with aileron but stick loads very heavy.
0.82 IMN	Alternate wing dropping. Ailerons not effective in controlling motion. Wing could be raised with rudder but on assuming level attitude the opposite wing dropped. Use of rudder produced snaking, which, with lateral motion, resulted in Dutch rolling. Longitudinal trim became nose up and heavy push force was required to hold dive. Marked buffeting.
0.83 IMN +	Complete loss of control and violent drop of either wing through 60–90 degrees. Ailerons quite ineffective and heavy. With roll, nose dropped and angle of dive became very steep. Buffeting and Dutch rolling in dive. Elevators only just effective, but application of small 'g' available increased buffeting and aircraft continued in dive. On occasions when 0.83 IMN was exceeded by making initial dive steep, aircraft became inverted when final wing drop occurred, and then nosed into very steep dive.

True Mach Number (TMN) was approximately 0.01 more than the Indicated Mach Number figures quoted above

In most cases recovery from the dive was made by closing the throttles and extending the airbrakes, the controls gradually becoming effective once again as the Mach number reduced. No adverse features were noted when the airbrakes were opened. On the return of aileron control it was possible to roll the aircraft into a laterally level attitude, but the stick forces required to do this were still heavy. In recovery the elevator was heavy, and because of the steep angle of dive and small reserve of 'g' available, the pull-out occupied considerable height. Some care was required during recovery to avoid entering a high-speed stall due to the small reserve of lift coefficient available at high Mach number.

When dives were entered at around 42,000–43,000 ft, recovery was usually complete by about 33,000 ft (no ventral tank), but with the ventral in place a further 3,000 ft was needed to attain level flight. On one occasion when flying without a ventral tank the airbrakes were not used, the pilot closing the throttles and recovering on elevator. In this instance recovery was very slow and level flight was not regained until 18,000 ft. The maximum TMN attained in the dives appeared to be about 0.85. Acceleration above 0.82 was slow and it was difficult to steepen the dive once the Mach number had risen appreciably above 0.81 due to loss of control effectiveness and response. Trim appeared to be nose up from 0.78 to 0.81 IMN, becoming nose down to 0.83 IMN and again nose up with any increase beyond 0.83 IMN. Dives were not carried out at lower level because of airframe deterioration.

It was concluded that there would be little point in exceeding the service limit of 0.78 IMN as the Meteor's efficiency as a gun platform deteriorated rapidly above 0.79–0.80 IMN due to the onset of buffeting and porpoising. It was also felt that a lack of manoeuvrability would make it difficult to set up attacks above 0.78 IMN. The only event in which a pilot might go above 0.78 IMN was in a breakaway manoeuvre or when taking evasive action, but any such manoeuvre leading to compressibility was likely to preclude further attacks.

With the arrival of the Meteor F.8 in 1950, the F.4 was gradually withdrawn from front-line squadrons but went on to give excellent service as single-seat trainers with Advanced Flying Schools until the advent of the Provost/Vampire sequence in 1954. The Meteor F.4 was also sold abroad and served with the air forces of Argentina, Belgium, Denmark, Egypt and the Netherlands.

CHAPTER 5

The Meteor F.8 Described

By the time that the Meteor F.8 entered RAF service with 245 Squadron at Horsham St Faith on 29 June 1950, the basic design had already been around for nearly ten years, George Carter having produced his preliminary brochure for what became the F.9/40 in August 1940. Unfortunately for the Meteor, what had seemed revolutionary just a few years before was now considered mundane, such had been the progress in aeronautics since the end of the Second World War. Although its conservative design meant that it was soon eclipsed by second-generation swept-wing fighters in the air combat role, its ruggedness was ideally suited to operations at low to medium levels. In this chapter it is proposed to take a closer look at the F.8, the ultimate single-seat Meteor.

STRUCTURE

The main components of the Meteor F.8 comprised the fuselage nose, the front and rear fuselage sections, a centre section (incorporating the centre fuselage), the outer planes and the tail unit. The front fuselage structure was based on two fore-and-aft diaphragms and four bulkheads, referred to as the nosewheel, seat, front tank and front spar bulkheads. The structure between the nosewheel and seat bulkheads was sealed to form the pressure cabin, which was completed by the armoured windscreen and the electrically operated sliding hood. The magazine bay was located between the seat and front tank bulkheads, and the front fuel tank was housed between the front tank and front spar bulkheads, the latter, together with the four longerons, being bolted to the centre fuselage. The fuselage centre and rear portions, which were joined at the longerons, were of semi-monocoque construction, the lower fin being an integral part of the rear fuselage tail portion.

The mainplanes were a two-spar, stressed-skin structure, the centre-section spars being interspersed by six major ribs, additional ribs of lighter construction being attached to the skin. Each engine nacelle was built around two main frames situated near the outer ends of the centre-section spars. The mainwheel bays, upper and lower airbrakes and the flaps were located between each nacelle and the centre fuselage. The outer planes, which were joined to the centre section at the spars, had plate and Warren girder ribs, and the internally mass-balanced ailerons were all-metal structures with automatic balance tabs.

The tail unit components were of all-metal, stressed-skin construction, the high position of the tailplane, necessitated by the hot air from the jet-pipes, dividing the rudder into two portions. The hydraulically operated undercarriage consisted of the nosewheel and two independent mainwheel units that retracted rearwards. The three units had levered-suspension legs with oleo-pneumatic shock absorber, the wheels being fitted with medium-pressure tyres. In addition to the normal electrical cockpit indicators, there was a mechanical down-lock indicator for the nosewheel showing forward of the windscreen. The stick-type control column and the parallel-acting rudder pedals were connected to the control surfaces by push-rods and cables with the trimming tabs on the tail unit being connected to their respective hand-wheels by chains and cables. Each engine was trunnion mounted between two centre-section ribs with bracing at the rear, and was served by an oil tank of twenty-two gallons capacity.

Services

Two accessory gearboxes (driving the generators, compressor, hydraulic and vacuum pumps) were mounted on the front spar and driven by extension shafts from the engines. The undercarriage, flaps and airbrakes were operated by a Dowty pump driven by the starboard accessory gearbox. These services could also be operated by a hand-pump, and there was also a compressed-air system for lowering the undercarriage in an emergency. A pneumatic system operated the mainwheel brakes and gun-cocking gear, the air container in the rear fuselage being charged by a Hymatic compressor on the port gearbox, or from an external supply.

The vacuum system comprised two pumps, one on each accessory gearbox, working the artificial horizon and (on early aircraft) the turn-and-slip indicator. Oxygen was carried in two 750-litre bottles in the magazine bay. The high-pressure supply was taken to a Mark 11C regulator that supplied an economiser on the port side of the seat. A flexible tube from the economiser was connected to the mask socket on the other side of the seat. Power for electrical services was supplied by two 24-volt, 3,000-watt engine-driven generators, charging two 12-volt accumulators. An electrical remote-control two-way radio and IFF apparatus were mounted in the rear fuselage.

Pressure cabin

The pressure cabin was supplied with heated air under pressure from the engines. Below 7,000 ft the system supplied only heat as the pressure cabin control valve automatically prevented any pressure building up, but above this height the air from the engines served the dual function of heating and pressurisation. The hood seal consisted of an inflatable rubber gasket held against the hood by a casting that extended round the windscreen arch, along the hood sills and behind the seat. Air to inflate the gasket was taken from the main supply pipe on the outlet side of the duplex non-return valve through a branch pipe. Cabin pressure was indicated in terms of equivalent altitude on the pressure cabin altimeter on the starboard panel in the cockpit. Readings were generally as follows:

Actual altitude	10,000 ft	20,000 ft	30,000 ft	40,000 ft
Equivalent cabin altitude	7,500 ft	13,000 ft	17,500 ft	23,000 ft

The full differential pressure of 3 lb/sq.in. was attained at 24,000 ft, and a horn behind the pilot's seat gave a warning of any dangerous drop in cabin pressure. When on the ground the hood could be pushed back by hand from the outside after it had been released from its operating mechanism by turning the external release handle. From the inside the hood was operated electrically by two push-buttons, but an internal release was provided so that it could also be hand operated.

FUEL SYSTEM

Fuel was carried in two fuselage tanks (a main tank in the centre fuselage and a front tank in the forward fuselage) and in three external tanks comprising a ventral tank under the fuselage and two wing drop tanks. The main tank was divided into two compartments by a transverse diaphragm, each compartment incorporating a fuel trap to permit inverted flight of short duration. Each compartment was connected by a gravity feed from the front tank and interconnected through a balance cock. Fuel was supplied to each engine, normally from the front compartment to the port (No. 1) engine and from the rear compartment to the starboard (No. 2) engine through a low-pressure cock. On the engine, the fuel passed through a low-pressure filter to the engine-driven pump, which supplied fuel at increased pressure to the burners through a throttle valve and a combined high-pressure cock and burner pressurising valve. Fuel was transferred from all the external tanks into the front tank by air pressure from the cabin pressure system. The rate of transfer was controlled by two float valves in the front tank (one for the wing tanks and one for the ventral), there being no cabin control. The relative levels of the valves ensured that the wing tanks emptied first.

GUNS

Four 20 mm Hispano guns were fitted in the front fuselage, two in each outer structure, mounted one above the other. To permit alignment of the belt-feed mechanism on each gun with its feed neck, the guns were staggered, the upper guns being approximately 10 in. aft of the lower guns. The belt-feed mechanisms were held in line with their feed necks by adjustable retention rods, the rear ends of each being bolted to the magazine carrier with the front end attached to the front mounting block. Ammunition tanks were situated inboard of the rear of the guns between the main fore-and-aft diaphragms that carried the tank support rails. Access to the tanks was obtained by lifting the rear end of the hood, which had to be securely locked by a jury strut. The ammunition load for each gun was 195 rounds, 160 of which were in the ammunition tank, with the remainder in the feed neck and belt-feed mechanism. Each gun was fed from a separate tank, the arrangement being port upper gun fed by rear lower tank, port lower gun fed by front lower tank, starboard upper gun fed by rear upper tank and starboard lower gun fed by front upper tank.

Each gun was fitted with a blast tube, the front end being screwed to the outer portion of the nosewheel bulkhead with the rear end as a push fit over the front gun-mounting ring. The port and starboard guns had independent heating systems. Hot air from a tapping at the bottom of each engine compressor casing was piped to a muff round the jet-pipe, which further heated the air, the pipe incorporating a pressure-relief valve that was set to blow at 30 lb/sq.in. From the muff the pipe continued to a temperature-control valve in the tank bay, hence the pipe extended forward into the front fuselage where it divided, each branch terminating in a fish-tail under the breech of each gun. Gun cocking was carried out pneumatically and firing electrically, a Maxiflux Star firing unit being fitted to each gun. Firing was controlled by a trigger on the control column. A Mark 4E gyro gunsight was fitted on a retractable mounting in the cockpit and a Type G45B cine camera was attached to a mounting on the nosewheel structure.

COCKPIT CONTROLS

Fuel cocks

The low- and high-pressure fuel cocks for each engine were located on either side of the pilot's seat and were marked LP and HP. The outer lever of each pair controlled the HP cock. The LP cocks cut off the flow of fuel from the main tank and were to be operated in the event of engine failure; however, they were not to be used to stop the engines as this might have damaged the fuel system. The HP cocks cut off the fuel supply to the engine burners, and these were used for stopping the engines (and also in the case of an engine failure). A balance cock on the cockpit floor aft of the rudder trimming-tab control was pulled up to interconnect the two compartments of the main fuel tank.

The ventral tank could be jettisoned by pulling a handle on the port side of the instrument panel, and the underwing tanks were jettisoned by moving the bomb/drop tank selector lever on the cockpit port side to the appropriate position. Two low-pressure pump circuit-breakers were located on the engine-starting panel on the cockpit port shelf, and these had to be switched to ON before the engines could be started. A panel below the instrument panel contained the three fuel gauges indicating the contents of the front tank and front and rear compartments of the main fuel tank.

Engine controls

The throttle levers were mounted in slides on the cockpit port wall, and when fully shut sufficient fuel was allowed to pass to enable the engine to idle. The starting cycle was controlled automatically by time switches. A shielded push-button on the port switch panel had to be pressed for about two seconds and then released. As soon as pressure on the push-buttons was released, the starter motors and torch igniters were brought into operation for the combustion process to begin. Current to the starter panel was automatically cut off after thirty seconds. For engine relights in the air, two push-buttons marked BOOST, TEST, PORT and STARBOARD were located at the top of the port switch panel and were used to energise the torch igniters. Engine instruments comprised RPM indicators, JPT gauges and oil-pressure gauges. The main ignition-isolating switch for each engine was fitted in the respective undercarriage bay. In the OFF position it isolated the boost coils and torch igniters from the starter panel and enabled the engine to be blown through using the normal starting gear after a false start.

Other essential controls

The rudder pedals could be adjusted for reach after pulling out a knob on the port side of the instrument panel to release the locking-mechanism. For trimming, the elevator and rudder trim tabs were controlled by hand-wheels on the port side of the cockpit, for which indicators were mounted alongside. The undercarriage was operated hydraulically by a selector lever on the port side of the instrument panel with two positions, UP and DOWN. It could not be set to UP while the weight of the aircraft was on the wheels, and there was no emergency override switch to enable the undercarriage to be raised on the ground. In the event of failure of the hydraulic pump and loss of accumulator pressure, or if No. 2 engine was not running, the undercarriage could be operated by a hand-pump or by the emergency air system. The undercarriage position indicators on the port side of the instrument panel operated as follows: undercarriage locked down – three greens; undercarriage between locks – three reds; undercarriage locked up – no lights. A warning light on the instrument panel came on if any wheel was not locked down and either throttle was less than one-third open. (At moderate to high altitudes the light tended to be on continuously, as the throttles were usually less than one-third open in cruising flight.) When the nosewheel was down and locked, a small rod protruded through the nose of the aircraft.

The flaps were operated hydraulically by a selector lever on the port side of the instrument panel. It had three positions, UP – NEUTRAL – DOWN. To obtain any intermediate position of the flaps, the lever had to be moved to DOWN, and when the flaps had reached the desired setting, the lever had to be returned to NEUTRAL. A flap-position indicator was mounted beside the undercarriage selector lever. Airbrakes were also operated hydraulically by a two-position selector lever on the port wall of the cockpit, marked ON in the aft position, and OFF in the forward position. Wheel braking was controlled by a lever incorporating a parking catch on the control column. Differential braking was controlled by the rudder pedals when the lever was depressed. The pneumatic pressure supply in the system and at each brake was shown on a triple pressure gauge. All three windscreen panels were heated electrically, the controlling switch for the port panel being located at the top of the panel, with the switch for the centre and starboard panels situated on the starboard coaming. A de-icing spray system was provided for the windscreen centre panel only, the de-icing hand-pump and flow control being mounted on the starboard wall of the cockpit.

Ejection seat

A Mark 1 ejection seat was fitted, incorporating a Type-ZA harness, harness release, head rest, two footrests and two thigh guards. At the rear of the seat was the ejection gun and on the port side of the seat the drogue gun. The ejection gun was fired by means of a handle immediately above the headrest to which was attached a flexible blind to protect the pilot's face. When the handle was pulled down to its full extent of its travel it released a sear that operated the firing pin. As the seat left the aircraft the emergency oxygen was turned on automatically. The drogue gun, which released a drogue parachute stowed in the container behind the pilot's headrest, was fired by means of a static line attached to the aircraft and was designed not to operate until the seat was well clear. The drogue parachute acted to slow down and stabilise the seat, enabling the pilot to release his harness, fall forward out of the seat and make a normal parachute descent.

The seat could be adjusted for height by means of a lever on the starboard side, the knob at the top of the lever being depressed and the lever moved in the natural sense to raise or lower the seat. The harness locks could be released by a spring-loaded lever on the starboard thigh guard, to allow the pilot to lean forward.

Emergency controls and equipment

The engine fire-extinguisher bottles located in the rear fuselage served spray rings at the rear of the engines and were operated electrically, either by two push-switches in the cockpit, or by an inertia switch in the starboard nacelle. The latter switch also cut out the remainder of the electrical services to minimise the risk of fire. Two fire-warning lamps, one for each engine, were mounted on the glare shields in the cockpit and were operated by flame switches in the nacelles.

The hydraulic hand-pump, located on the starboard side of the seat, had a telescopic handle by which the pilot could operate any of the hydraulic services, i.e. undercarriage, flaps and airbrakes, after the appropriate selector lever had been moved. The compressed-air system to lower the undercarriage in an emergency was operated by a T-handle on the starboard cockpit wall, there being no need to move the selector lever. The T-handle had to be pulled to its full extent to allow a spring-loaded plunger to engage and hold the handle in the operating position.

For emergency lighting, an emergency lamp on the port glare shield was controlled by a switch on the starboard side of the cockpit, power being supplied from an alkaline accumulator under the starboard decking. An IFF distress switch was located on the starboard switch panel, and in an emergency the gyro gunsight could be lowered manually by pushing the red knob below the sight.

For situations involving lack of oxygen, pulling a knob on the starboard cockpit wall connected the emergency oxygen cylinder (carried in the dinghy pack) to the pilot's mask. The force required to pull the knob was such that the possibility of accidental operation was negligible. Provision was made for the pilot to carry a Type-K dinghy. In emergency situations the hood could be jettisoned by pulling a spade grip at the top of the starboard instrument panel. This opened the side rails to free the side runners, the rear runner automatically disengaging itself as the hood swung up.

CHAPTER 6

Trials with the Meteor F.8

The Meteor F.8 was also tested at CFE in 1950, and two early production Gloster-built aircraft (VZ443 and VZ508) were delivered to West Raynham, together with VZ530 from the Armstrong Whitworth production line at Baginton. The cockpit layout of the F.8 showed a number of improvements over the F.4. In general it was considered to be roomy, well laid out and presenting no difficulty for quick entry. The instrument layout was improved, the flap and undercarriage levers in particular being easier to operate. There was also improved cockpit heating and a modified heating system for the guns. The stick-pattern control column was a considerable improvement and the camera button was much easier to use. One negative aspect, however, was that the thigh guards of the Martin Baker ejection seat made it more difficult to use the elevator trimmer and to see the rudder trim indicators.

The hood was operated electrically by two push-buttons, taking around four to five seconds to close and eight to eleven seconds to open. This was considered to be an excessively long time, especially when a quick scramble was required. Like the F.4, the hood jettison lever was badly placed as it was out of sight and would probably have proved to be difficult to operate if the aircraft was under any 'g' loading. The engine relight switches on the F.8 remained in a position that was not easily accessible, and as with the F.4 relighting was a difficult procedure. The opinion was expressed that repositioning of the relight buttons on the HP cock levers would have been a great improvement.

Pilots used to the Meteor F.4 found that they were sitting slightly further back in the cockpit of the F.8, and they were particularly appreciative of the improved blind-flying panel with G4F compass and electric turn and slip. A vacuum pump was also fitted to each engine so that in the event of failure of one of the pumps (or when flying on one engine) the second pump automatically served the artificial horizon, which was now the only suction-driven instrument on the panel. The retractable gyro gunsight fitted above the instrument panel was normally retained in the lowered position during the search phase of an interception (but with the GGS circuit-breaker switch to ON). On making visual contact, the sight was raised electrically, the operation taking around three seconds. In the event of failure of the electrical system, there was no manual way of lifting the sight. If a failure occurred after the sight had been raised it could be lowered in emergency by pushing a red knob on the starboard side of the sight.

With the fuselage of the F.8 lengthened by thirty inches, this allowed an additional fuel tank containing 95 gallons to be installed forward of the main tanks and for the elimination of all but 176 lb of ballast. The take-off characteristics of the F.8 were similar to its predecessor, and no difficulty was experienced in taking-off with a mixed formation of F.4s and F.8s. The initial acceleration of the F.8 appeared slightly slower than the F.4, although the impression was also gained that the lift-off was a little cleaner and at a slower speed. There was consequently no increase in take-off distance, and it was possible for a fully loaded aircraft fitted with a ventral tank to become airborne in a little over 700 yards in conditions of no wind. This was achieved by building up to full power against the brakes at the end of the runway and selecting thirty degrees of flap. It was found that the new rudder gave better directional control, and as the rudder forces were lighter, this reduced the minimum speed for safe control in the event of an engine failure by 15 knots to 135 kts IAS. For take-off, however, the safety speed remained at 150 kts IAS.

When climbing to achieve best range, endurance or the shortest time to height, it was found to be important to climb at high rpm. Overall, the rate of climb and time to height for the F.8 were very similar to the figures recorded by the F.4. In terms of speed the F.8 was an improvement on the F.4 in that the limiting Mach number had been increased by 0.02, giving an increase of about 12 kts IAS. This was only an advantage in straight and level flight above 35,000 ft, however, as below this height the increase could not be exploited, except in a dive, as there was no extra power available. Above 35,000 ft the increase could be utilised, as at these altitudes the F.4 was limited in speed by Mach number and not by power available. A Meteor F.8 in clean configuration stalled at 125 kts IAS at 40,000 ft, and the carriage of a ventral tank increased the stalling speed by about 5 kts IAS. As the stalling speed of the F.8 was 5 kts IAS higher than the F.4, the absolute speed range (stall to limiting Mach number) was about the same for the two aircraft.

Although there was little difference in speed between the F.4 and the F.8, the latter was more pleasant at high speed, particularly at Mach numbers in excess of 0.76. Unlike the F.4, there was no tendency to pitch as compressibility was approached, and consequently there was no difficulty in sighting with the F.8 right up to critical Mach. In terms of acceleration there was little to choose between the two except that the F.8 appeared to be slightly superior above 40,000 ft. However, there was a marked difference when it came to deceleration as the airbrakes of the F.4 did not open fully at speeds above about 365 kts IAS. In the F.8, larger hydraulic jacks allowed the airbrakes to be opened fully up to 490 kts IAS. At low level this could be a particular advantage if it was necessary to make a quick turn of comparatively small radius during evasive action or after sighting a target, particularly in poor visibility. Any use of airbrakes above 450 kts IAS was accompanied by buffeting and yawing and a marked nose-down change of trim. The rate of deceleration was very rapid, and speed could be reduced from 490 to 350 kts in nine seconds.

Turning rates and radii at all heights were similar, although it was considered that the F.4 might have had a slight advantage. As already mentioned, the F.8 could out-turn an F.4 at high speed and low level thanks to its superior airbrakes. No improvement was noted in the early production F.8s as far as rolling performance was concerned, and at high speed lateral control remained exceedingly heavy. Later, an improvement did come about with the introduction of spring-tab ailerons as replacements for the geared tabs fitted to early aircraft. In general the flying qualities of the F.8 were considered an improvement. Rudder forces were lighter and the elevators were more pleasant, but there was a noticeable tendency to 'snake' both at slow speeds and with the airbrakes extended. This tendency became less at high speed. Although larger variations of trim were required with change of speed and throttle setting, the trimmers were more positive in action.

All fighter aircraft are judged on speed and manoeuvrability – i.e. their ability to turn, roll, climb, dive, accelerate and decelerate. In most of these respects the F.4 and F.8 were similar, but while higher speeds were possible with the F.8, its slightly higher wing loading and stalling speed meant that it was consequently a little less manoeuvrable than the F.4 at all altitudes. Rearward vision was also a problem in that the solid metal portion at the rear of the canopy produced a blind area of about twenty degrees in the 6 o'clock position. This was considered unacceptable, and later aircraft were to appear with a full-blown canopy. However, the F.8 was considered an improvement in terms of forward vision, thanks to its retractable gyro gunsight, the repositioning of the Machmeter on the instrument panel, improved cabin heating, which reduced external frosting, and the positioning of the cockpit further forward of the wings and engine nacelles.

For recovery to base, although best range could be achieved in the descent by throttling back and flying at high speed, this method was often not possible due to operational restrictions. It was also not particularly desirable from the pilot's point of view, as extremely high rates of descent could be achieved by extending the airbrakes and diving the aircraft at speeds slightly below limiting Mach. Even with cabin pressurisation, a descent of this kind was extremely uncomfortable. The recommended fast descent prior to an instrument procedure was the same as in the Meteor F.4 – i.e. 230 kts IAS and 11,000 rpm with airbrakes extended. The time taken for a descent from 40,000 ft to ground level in this case was around six minutes.

The actual landing was similar to the F.4, and both aircraft had a maximum landing weight of 14,700 lb. As the F.8 was the heavier by about 500 lb, with a ventral tank fitted 325 gallons would normally have to be used before landing, leaving 270 gallons remaining. A clean F.8 was not to be landed when more than 350 gallons remained, or, if full ammunition was being carried, when more than 300 gallons remained. The increased fuel capacity of the F.8 allowed much greater operational flexibility, and with a ventral tank installed, the F.8's total fuel capacity was 595 gallons. This allowed an increase in endurance of up to twenty to thirty minutes. Below 25,000 ft an increase in range could be achieved by shutting-down one engine. This advantage decreased with altitude from a twenty-three per cent improvement at sea level to no benefit at 25,000 ft. When flying for range on one engine, optimum cruising speed was about 20 kts IAS slower than the optimum for flight on two engines.

Although the Meteor F.8 had demonstrated some significant improvements over the F.4, the CFE report had to concede that many of its advantages were negated by operational difficulties with the Rolls-Royce Derwent 8 engines. Problems were experienced with overheating at full power over 30,000 ft, and on occasions surging was also encountered. The inability to use full power at height was a most serious restriction and was considered to be 'quite unacceptable' in a fighter aircraft. Subsequent modifications to production aircraft rectified most of the snags experienced during the trial, which was carried out in summer conditions.

CHAPTER 7

Meteors over Korea

Although the Meteor never encountered the Messerschmitt Me 262 in the Second World War, jet-versus-jet air combat was not long in coming. The invasion of South Korea by North Korean forces on 25 June 1950 found 77 Squadron, Royal Australian Air Force, at Iwakuni in Japan as part of the British Commonwealth Occupation Forces flying Australian-built P-51 Mustangs. Coming under the operational control of the US 5th Air Force, the unit was ordered to prepare for immediate action, and on 2 July its Mustangs flew as cover for USAF B-29s attacking an airfield at Yongpu, near Hamhung. Operations from Korean bases were to follow, but in late April 1951 the squadron returned to Iwakuni to re-equip with Meteor F.8s, which had arrived by aircraft carrier from the UK.

Following its work-up period, 77 Squadron flew to its new base at Kimpo, near Seoul, and began the daily grind of fighter sweeps and bomber escort missions in 'MiG Alley'. Many of the pilots had mixed feelings about the Meteor; some were reluctant to say goodbye to their Mustangs and others had hoped that they might get Sabres. Their misgivings were to be vindicated during the first real test against the MiG-15 on 29 August 1951. The subsequent Intelligence Report describes the action:

Anzac Item Flight		Anzac Dog Flight	
1 – S/L D.L. Wilson	A77-616	1 – F/O G. Thornton	A77-741
2 – Sgt N.M. Woodruffe	A77-811	2 – Sgt E.D. Armitt	A77-949
3 – F/L C.G. Thomas	A77-959	3 – Sgt K.H. Foster	A77-728
4 – F/O K.J. Blight	A77-559	4 – W/O R.D. Guthrie	A77-721

Pilots were briefed to carry out a fighter sweep in the Chongju area, in conjunction with sixteen F-86 aircraft. Each aircraft was armed with full loads of 20 mm ammunition. They were airborne under the callsigns of Anzac Item and Dog in two flights of four aircraft each.

After being cleared by 'Snowflake' (control), the sweep commenced with the Meteors flying at 35,000 ft. At 1120 hrs over 'YE5070', two flights of six MiG-15 aircraft were observed heading west at 40,000 ft. Item Flight turned left to keep them in sight and sighted two more MiGs at 30,000 ft. Item 1 and 2 dived to attack. The MiGs dived and pulled slightly to the left. Item 2 spun in the dive and dropped out of the fight. Item 1 opened fire with unobserved results and immediately felt hits on his own aircraft. Item 1 broke away. Item 3 and 4 dived on the MiG attacking Item 1 and fired with unobserved results. The MiG broke and dived away. At 1126 hrs Item 3 sighted four MiGs and made a firing pass at the number 4, again without result.

At 1123 hrs over 'YD1090', four MiG-15s attacked Dog Flight. The leader called break and when the flight levelled out Dog 4 was missing. Dog leader called Dog 4 and Item 1 answered at 1125 hrs to say he could see a parachute at 'XE8030'. F-86 aircraft in the area later reported a Meteor smoking and spinning at about that time. No F-86 aircraft were lost in the encounter and no enemy aircraft were claimed damaged or destroyed. Dog leader called an amphibious rescue aircraft orbiting over the west coast of Korea but could not make contact until 1145 hrs.

On return to base, Item 3 observed an unidentified aircraft crash about 30 miles south-east of Kimpo. This crash could not be investigated due to lack of fuel. Aircraft A77-616 landed with the port aileron destroyed and the main fuel tank punctured from above. The bullet was lodged in the tank.

The pilot shot down was Warrant Officer R.D. Guthrie, who successfully ejected from his crippled aircraft and was taken prisoner. Another major air battle took place on 5 September, which once again underlined the MiG-15's superiority and a high degree of tactical skill on the part of the MiG pilots:

Anzac Able Flight		Anzac Baker Flight	
1 – F/L V.B. Cannon	A77-189	1 – F/O G. Thornton	A77-741
2 – Sgt E.J. Myers	A77-464	2 – Sgt M.E. Colebrook	A77-368
3 – F/L C.I. Blyth	A77-385	3 – F/L R.L. Dawson	A77-163
4 – Sgt E.D. Armitt	A77-949	4 – W/O W.S. Michelson	A77-726

Pilots were briefed to provide close escort to two RF-80s from a rendezvous over Tan-do to a target in the Sinuiju area. Each aircraft was armed with full loads of 20 mm ammunition. They were airborne under the callsigns of Anzac Able and Baker in two flights of four aircraft.

After being cleared by 'Shirley' (control), two aircraft aborted, one with inoperative guns and one escorted him back to base. Rendezvous was established with the RF-80s but after one RF-80 had made two passes he returned to base. The other RF-80 was in the target area for about 17–18 minutes and covered the railway line from Sonchon to Chungju. At 1735 hrs twelve MiG-15s were sighted at 26,000 ft (2,000 ft above the Meteors) heading 310 degrees on a reciprocal course. The MiGs flew past the Meteors, turned 180 degrees and attacked from 6 o'clock high. Combat discipline was very good. Six MiGs came down first and friendly fighters broke left. The MiGs followed round in pairs, two would fire then pull up, second pair would fire then pull up, third pair would fire then pull up, all in formation. While the first six drew off and regrouped, the second six would come in and repeat the tactics of the first group.

The encounter lasted 5–6 minutes, during which Able 1 and 3 fired two bursts each with no observed result. Baker 4 fired one burst then received a hit which threw him on his back and the aircraft went into a long dive out of control. The pilot could see that his tail assembly was damaged and made no attempt to pull out too quickly, or to use speed brakes, for fear of applying strain to the damaged part. The aircraft gradually flattened out and the pilot was able to regain control at 10,000 ft. Baker 4 received major damage to his port tailplane. When the first group of six MiGs drew off to regroup, Able 3 observed one to be emitting white smoke. No claims are made pending camera gun results. MiG aircraft appeared to turn tighter and pull up faster than the Meteors and were considerably faster.

Following these engagements, 77 Squadron's CO, Wg Cdr Gordon Steege DSO DFC, produced an unfavourable tactical report on the Meteor's qualities in comparison with the MiG-15, concluding that it was 'vastly inferior in performance'. In part his report read as follows:

Limiting Mach Number – the limiting Mach 0.82 of the Meteor is so much lower than that of the MiG (at least 0.90) that it is a handicap of considerable magnitude. This handicap means that the MiG invariably has the initiative in regard to attack and breaking off attack. It cruises operationally at a Mach number well above that at which the Meteor is in compressibility and as it has superior height performance the Meteor's tactics will invariably be defensive manoeuvrability in the level plane. If the MiG chooses to dive away the Meteor's limiting Mach number prohibits it following down. In fact all the MiG has to do is to fly around the area at Mach 0.80+ and it need not even take avoiding action as far as the Meteor is concerned. When MiGs have been attacked by Meteors as they pulled away, smart reverse action on the ranging drum of the reflector sight has been necessary to keep the aircraft 'nipped' at the rate of opening – rather than closing.

Visibility – in an aircraft which must invariably expect the initial attack to be delivered rather than deliver it, the [rearward] visibility limitation is serious. This disconcerting feature of the Meteor was the subject of much bitter comment at the recent RAF Fighter Convention from the AOC-in-C down. Attention was drawn to the excellent visibility from American and Russian fighter cockpits. [This point was later refuted by the Chief of the Air Staff, Air Chief Marshal Sir John Slessor in a memo to his counterpart in the RAAF, Air Marshal George Jones, in which he claimed that the criticism of the Meteor in this respect at a recent CFE convention referred to the Meteor night-fighter and not the F.8.]

Employment of the Meteor – the above is not a very bright picture but the fact must be faced that unless the MiGs are operated unintelligently, Meteors are not going to account for many. Further, relative results may be such that the employment of the Meteor in a more economical role may have to be considered. However, for the time being it is planned that they will concentrate on bomber escort. When used on fighter sweeps they will fly in very close co-ordination with F-86 formations with a view to exploiting the manoeuvrability and zoom features against MiGs which have been attacked by F-86 formations and cannot dive away, but must manoeuvre or pull up. Nevertheless this co-ordination will not be easy, for in the words of a USAF colonel, in the MiG area F-86 pilots 'ride the Mach', and the Mach they ride is considerably higher than that of the Meteor.

The views as expressed by Wg Cdr Steege were echoed by several of his pilots to the extent that they became known to journalists covering the war and formed the basis for newspaper reports highlighting the Meteor's deficiencies. These came at a particularly bad time as Gloster had been actively promoting the Meteor in the air defence role and there was the prospect of selling more aircraft to NATO air forces and other air arms around the world. A memo from AM Jones to ACM Sir John Slessor spoke of 'far-reaching consequences' of the newspaper talk, and that the whole issue was likely to become a 'politically hot question'. The tactics employed by 77 Squadron came in for close scrutiny, in particular the fact that on a number of occasions the Meteors appeared to be flying top cover at 30,000–35,000 ft with formations of F-86 Sabres at 25,000 ft. To this, Slessor had written the single word 'stupid' on Steege's report. In slightly more underhand fashion, comments were made noting that Steege rarely flew with the squadron, and questions were also asked as to the unit's morale.

The Americans were generally sympathetic to the Meteor's problems, and the commander of Far Eastern Air Forces, Lt Gen O.P. 'Opie' Weyland, expressed his views in correspondence with Maj Gen Leon W. Johnson, who, among other duties, was head of the Military Assistance Advisory Group for the UK. Weyland noted the undesirable implications of changing Meteor operations, since a number of NATO nations were depending upon the aircraft for air defence purposes, and the implications of a 'bad name' applied to the aeroplane could have been serious.

He went on to state:

> We feel no particular concern about operating the F-80 and F-84 in the areas of MiG activity although they are no match in speed with the MiG and definitely cannot engage in air combat on even terms. By the same token the Meteor is also no match for the MiG in speed, but it does have a number of characteristics which could be used to advantage in combat with the MiGs. These are its good rate of turn, its excellent climb and excellent armament. I frankly do not feel that these good characteristics were fully developed in the very limited engagements with MiG-15s. In any event I do not think that the airplane should in any way be damned because of its performance in the Korean theatre. It is a short-legged airplane built for air defence purposes and I believe it is a good one for this purpose.

No. 77 Squadron was to encounter MiG-15s on a regular basis for the rest of the war, one of the biggest air battles occurring on 1 December 1951. On this day twelve Meteors took off from Kimpo for a fighter sweep and met a formation of around fifty MiGs. With height advantage, the MiGs dived on the Meteors, and A77-559, flown by Flt Sgt W. Middlemiss, was severely damaged and forced to return to base. In the midst of the mêlée Flg Off Bruce Gogerly (A77-17) found himself in a good position and fired a long burst of cannon fire into a MiG-15, hitting it along the fuselage and wing root. This aircraft was seen to crash in flames and it thus became 77 Squadron's first confirmed MiG kill. A second MiG went down having been hit by fire from several aircraft. Despite the fact that all remaining Meteors had acknowledged the call to return to base, after landing it was discovered that three pilots were missing. It later transpired that Sgts Vance Drummond (A77-251) and Bruce Thompson (A77-29) had been forced to eject to become PoWs, and Sgt Ernest Armitt (A77-949) had been killed.

With the arrival of a new CO, in the person of Wg Cdr Ron Susans DSO DFC, at the end of December, 77 Squadron's role became much more ground-attack orientated, and the unit's Meteors were soon fitted with underwing rockets featuring an Australian-developed napalm warhead. The dangers of low-level attack were quickly demonstrated, however, and in March 1952 Sgts I. Cranston

(A77-920) and L. Cowper (A77-120) were both shot down and killed by flak. To try to counter the Meteors' activities, MiG-15s were committed further south, and on 4 May Plt Off J. Surman was credited with a probable in a brief exchange near Pyongyang. As these engagements were now taking place at lower altitudes, the performance gap between the Meteor and the MiG was less pronounced, and on 8 May Plt Off Bill Simmonds (A77-385) claimed a MiG-15 whose pilot was seen to eject while in a spin. The MiGs were to gain revenge on 2 October when Plt Off O. Cruickshank, RAF, was shot down and killed in A77-436 when he was jumped on returning from a ground attack mission.

The last encounter with the MiGs occurred on 27 March 1953 during an armed reconnaissance by four Meteors in the area around Pyongyang. Splitting into pairs, Wg Cdr John Hubble AFC and Flt Lt Rees swung north from a road junction at Namch'onjom, while Sgts George Hale and Dave Irlam headed south. Not long after, Hale and Irlam spotted two RF-80s being followed by a pair of MiG-15s. As his aircraft was fitted with two rocket projectiles, Hale fired these at the nearest MiG, giving its pilot an almighty fright and prompting him to climb and head for home. Irlam than called to say that he had been hit, and Hale became aware of two more MiGs diving out of the sun. One advantage that the Meteor possessed over the MiG-15 was its ability to decelerate rapidly, thanks to extremely effective airbrakes, and Hale was able to cause the MiG to overshoot. Kicking on left rudder, he fired a short burst and saw strikes just behind the cockpit, which produced a plume of black smoke. The MiG then fell away and went straight down. He was not able to follow as he was attacked by two more and forced to turn into them. As he was firing at these, another pair sliced down onto him, so he turned in behind them and secured hits on one, which caused a stream of white smoke to be emitted from its jet-pipe. By now Hale was out of ammunition, so he disengaged and dived back to Kimpo. He was able to do this in relative safety as Hubble and Rees had arrived by this time, prompting the rest of the MiGs to head north. Although his aircraft was riddled with bullet holes, Dave Irlam made it safely back to base and Hale was later awarded with one probable and a damaged.

By the time that the armistice came into effect on 27 June 1953, 77 Squadron had destroyed 1,500 vehicles, twenty locomotives, sixty-five railway carriages, sixteen bridges and 3,700 buildings. Out of a total of 18,872 sorties, 15,000 had been flown in Meteors. Three MiG-15s were claimed destroyed, but this overall effort had to be set against the loss of forty-two pilots, thirty-two of them while flying Meteors.

CHAPTER 8

Flying Tiger

The first production Meteor F.8 (VZ438) was delivered to the RAF on 10 December 1949, and this variant was to remain as Fighter Command's principal single-seat day interceptor until 1955, by which time the early versions of the Hawker Hunter were entering service. In all, nineteen squadrons flew the Meteor F.8, plus another ten squadrons of the Royal Auxiliary Air Force. No. 74 'Tiger' Squadron began its association with the Meteor in May 1945 when it converted from the Spitfire LF.16e to the Meteor F.3, and by the early 1950s it was flying the F.8 from Horsham St Faith near Norwich. Alan Colman joined the squadron in July 1952 – he recalls his introduction to squadron life and some of his experiences as a fighter pilot:

I joined 74 Squadron as a brand new pilot officer straight out of OCTU. Norwich was my home town and I had managed to get myself posted to Horsham St Faith on compassionate grounds as my mother's health had been badly affected by the recent death of my father. I therefore 'lived out' at Old Catton, which was only a few hundred yards from the airfield. As a sergeant pilot I had converted onto the Meteor F.4 and T.7 and attended the Fighter Command OCU in 1951 while on my National Service. I then left the RAF, rejoining in March 1952 and eventually arriving at Horsham not having flown a Meteor of any sort for a year and never having flown a Meteor F.8. This outraged Major Milholland, the USAF exchange officer who was the Squadron CO at the time. He immediately tried to persuade Fighter Command to post me elsewhere. Luckily for me he was unsuccessful, but in an effort to achieve his aim through other means, he gave me a desperately hard time for my first few months.

I was saved by the 'A' Flight commander, Flt Lt Joe Maddison, who had been an instructor at 205 AFS, Middleton St George, where I had carried out my original Meteor conversion in early 1951. Joe volunteered to take me under his wing, renew my 'instrument rating' and bring me up to operational standard using the Station Flight Meteor T.7. This he did, but it did not save me from being intimidated by the 'boss', and he regularly contrived to make me look a fool in front of the rest of the squadron. Due to an accident that had killed one of the students on my course at the OCU at Stradishall, we had passed out without having undertaken any air-to-air firing practice. Consequently, my total inexperience in air gunnery and poor results provided him with rich source for complaint and ridicule, but he also objected because, unlike most of his other junior pilots, I didn't live in the mess and so missed out on some of the social life of the squadron. Later on, perhaps stung by his carping criticism, I became one of the highest gunnery scorers on the squadron and 'a bit of an ace' at formation flying and mock dogfighting – thereby achieving full acceptance as 'one of the boys'.

Air firing proficiency was something of an obsession on the squadron at that time, and 74 had a very high reputation in Fighter Command as the 1952 winner of the annual trophy awarded to the highest scoring squadron, then called the Dacre Trophy. Not surprisingly in the above circumstances, the real highlight of the squadron year was the annual detachment to the Armament Practice Camp (APC) at RAF Acklington in Northumberland. The entire squadron went on these detachments – aircraft, ground support, fuel bowsers, everything! Car ownership was very rare among squadron aircrew in those days, so as the owner of a three-wheeled and motorcycle-engined Bond Minicar I was detailed as OC of the 1953 squadron MT convoy, which I led in this small and fundamentally unreliable contraption all the 300 miles from Norfolk to Northumberland.

At these APCs we had a chance to fire on our usual 'flag' targets and also on glider targets towed by Tempests. The big difference was that the targets were towed at 20,000 ft instead of the 7,000 ft or so which was the upper limit on our home firing-range off the Norfolk coast near Yarmouth. The extra altitude made a huge difference to the handling of the Meteor during the standard very close-in and abbreviated 'high quarter' type of attack we used (experience had demonstrated that the highest scores were obtained by using very short bursts of gunfire – requiring a large number of firing passes to expend all of your ammunition). I well remember one occasion when, a hundred feet from the target, my aircraft suddenly flick-rolled out of control due to compressibility effects just as I had started to fire. Helpless, I watched in terror as I hurtled inverted over the top of the 'flag', missing it by about six feet.

On another occasion I carefully emptied every round of 20 mm ammunition I carried into a 'glider' target, only to see it fly on serenely and, apparently, undamaged. Determined to see if I had hit it at all, I approached the glider intending to formate on it to have a look. Just as I was easing into position the glider fell apart before my eyes, leaving nothing behind the Tempest but the tow rope. However, my biggest air-firing drama had nothing to do with gunnery skill or handling qualities. Having completed my initial turn in during a 'quarter attack' on another glider target, I was tracking the glider through my gunsight when, without any warning from the tug pilot or the GCI radar that was supposed to be watching us, a giant American ten-engined Convair B-36 bomber suddenly filled my windscreen, passing straight through my line of fire. Half a second later and I would have either collided with the bomber or shot it down!

So soon after the war there was still a powerful 'gung-ho' attitude, and 'flying the aircraft to its limits' was a much more powerful motivation than flight safety, which was then a new and suspiciously unmilitary concept. The maintenance and display of the aggressive operating reputation of the squadron was paramount. The rules controlling our flying were, compared with those existing today, very flexible, and 'cowboy' operation was tacitly encouraged if it produced the desired publicity! The citizens of Hellesdon, who lived under the flightpath of the then main Horsham St Faith runway, became very hostile at what they saw as the irresponsible behaviour of the pilots of the Horsham Wing. Letters appeared in the press and we were confidentially advised not to be seen in the Hellesdon area in uniform.

The cause of the problem was primarily the greatly increased noise footprint and speed of jet aircraft when compared to that of their piston-engined forerunners at Horsham. This characteristic was exacerbated by the requirement to repeatedly practise squadron and wing take-offs, sometimes involving around thirty aircraft in pairs or fours, rolling at five- or ten-second intervals. Inevitably, alternate sections had to stay low initially to avoid the slipstream of the aircraft immediately ahead. Attempts to offset this adverse local reaction were made, and Flg Off Derek Morter and myself (both local boys) were featured in the East Anglian press in an article entitled 'Men With Thunder Under Their Gloves'. My main recollection of Derek was his return to base one day with the underside of his Meteor scratched and dented. The front of the ventral tank was punctured and there were twigs erupting from it! On an Army Co-operation exercise he had hit a tree in the Thetford battle area while trying to frighten the forward air controller into abandoning his Land Rover. [For a full description of this incident see p. 128].

One of the pilots on 74 Squadron was a likeable extrovert called Gus Napier who made his mark immediately by arriving in a gorgeous SS100 Jaguar sports car. Gus was a hard man, and he specialised in display aerobatics, particularly gut-wrenching high 'g' manoeuvres, such as the 'square loop'. Gus was selected to display the Meteor at the Battle of Britain show at Horsham St Faith (in the early 1950s there was a display at almost every active RAF station every year). As usual, Gus hurtled back and forth across the airfield, performing an immaculate series of conventional aerobatics, but he finished off with his star-turn 'square loop'. This involved very high 'g' at the corners and a short period of level inverted flying at the top. It was very noisy, not only due to the high power settings required, but also there was thunderous aerodynamic noise as the airframe was pushed into the buffet boundary. It was very impressive to hear and to watch. When Gus landed, however, it was clear that his Meteor F.8 had not enjoyed the experience. Huge wrinkles could be seen, like bow waves from a boat, where the centre section joined the fuselage and also along the wing itself. The OC Tech Wing was called and declared the aircraft Category 5 (scrap), and we never saw it again. I do not remember anyone even thinking of disciplining the pilot: instead, he was congratulated on a brilliant display. How times have changed!

In addition to our normal training, we also had to take part in the occasional mass flypast, such as that for the Queen's birthday. In those days each squadron had twenty-two aircraft, and each Fighter Command station had two squadrons in its wing. On such occasions it was normal for each squadron to put up at least twelve aircraft, so each wing consisted of twenty+. These wing formations then wheeled around over the Thames Estuary, forming up in threes to produce an impressive wave formation of some seventy-two aircraft. There would be several of these unwieldy wave formations in line astern to make up the Fighter Command contribution – literally hundreds of Meteors blasting down the Thames in close formation. It was a wonderful and stirring sight and sound, but a nightmare to time, organise and form up. It was also an extremely exhausting bit of flying for the pilots – the bigger the formation the more difficult the station keeping, especially in mid-summer turbulence and temperatures. In practice for one of these flypasts, the Horsham formation lost its wing leader, Wg Cdr Bob Yule. His Meteor's tail was knocked off by his No. 4 when there was a sudden call for the formation to pull up to avoid collision with a Hurricane which was running late and out of position [this incident occurred on 11 September 1953; Yule's Meteor F.8, WF695, crashed at Woolwich in south-east London]. The huge block of Meteors, of course, were among the fastest aircraft in the display, and their run-in had to be timed very precisely so that the older and slower aircraft had just cleared the focal point (usually

Buckingham Palace) before they arrived.

We were also required to send sixteen Meteor F.8s from 74 Squadron to Hooton Park in order to carry out a formation flypast over Liverpool. On this occasion I was to fly as No. 4 ('in the box') in the rearmost section of four. Consequently, I was flying at a lower level than any of the other aircraft in the formation. About half-way round the flypast route, low over the Mersey, my aircraft was viciously attacked by a seagull. It hit the nose just below the windscreen, making a small hole, most of its entrails entering the cockpit, while much of the blood flowed over the windscreen and the canopy. It was instant, total, red-out, and I was immediately forced to abandon my formation position as I could not see anything looking forward. The smell inside the cockpit was revolting, and I was pleased to open the canopy. I made a successful landing off a curved approach with my goggled head sticking out of the side to see where I was going.

Apart from the annual visit to APC at Acklington, there were other regular events which dominated squadron life. One of these was the rotating requirement to mount the Immediate Readiness flight. In those days this was called Operation Fabulous. It required a flight of four fully armed aircraft with pilots to be on immediate standby from one hour before sunrise to one hour after sunset. The first and last hour required the pilots to be in their cockpits with their headsets plugged in to the sector controller via 'telescramble'. 'Fabulous' came round several times a year and tied up aircraft and crews for a week at a time. If there was no 'trade' (i.e. no unidentified aircraft over the North Sea to be investigated), it was normal for the Fabulous aircraft to be periodically allowed 'off the hook' to fly for training. This flying was normally utilised for practice interceptions, but on special occasions it was used for other purposes, such as 'bombing' the Coltishall Station Commander's married quarters with toilet rolls at dawn on Christmas Day! The toilet rolls were transported by trapping them in the flaps and released by momentarily selecting 'flaps down'.

Another regular annual event was the station inspection by the AOC of 12 Group. At the time the AOC was that famous and eccentric Air Force character, AVM R.L.R. 'Batchy' Atcherley. One of these inspections sticks in my memory. It was in mid-winter and we had held the usual practice parades with our greatcoats on. However, on the day, we were told that officers were to parade in their No. 1 uniforms, but with no coats on – the reason given was that the AOC did not have one! It was a clear and frosty morning and we stood on parade shivering, waiting for the AOC to arrive by air. After about fifteen minutes a Meteor arrived in the Horsham circuit at high speed, made a spectacular break onto the downwind leg and lowered the undercarriage. At that point an American F-84 Thunderjet appeared and 'bounced' the Meteor as it turned finals. The Meteor immediately broke off its landing approach, raised its undercarriage and proceeded to chase the Thunderjet. Round and round the two aircraft twisted above our freezing heads until, at last, the American pilot gave up and set off for his own base. The Meteor landed, out climbed a red-faced and perspiring AOC and the inspection proceeded as if nothing had happened!

The annual summer exercise saw both Horsham squadrons (Nos 74 and 245) dispersed to the extremities of the airfield, with ground staff and crews living in tents. It was always good fun and an excuse to demonstrate just how fast the squadron could scramble, and how tenacious the pilots could be in making a successful interception. For instance, it provided an excuse for the Station Commander to demonstrate his prowess by taking off from the perimeter track and for me to jump into a Meteor that was in the middle of being serviced, only to be stopped by an airman shoving his head into the cockpit and shouting, 'You 'aint got no radio sir, did you know?' Targets ranged from very-high-flying Canberras and B-47s, through B-29s at medium level and down to very-low-flying Thunderjets and Venoms. Another favourite was the convoy patrol, which usually involved a vicious tangle with Fleet Air Arm Sea Furies low over the sea. Most of our attempts to intercept really high-flying raiders were doomed to failure because, although we could often see our target, we just did not have a sufficient performance margin to both climb up to its level and catch it before getting low on fuel and having to return to base. I have much more vivid memories of practice interceptions on B-29s and Sea Furies.

One of the senior pilots on the squadron was Flt Lt Bertie Beard. As a new pilot I clearly remember flying as his No. 2 as he led the squadron on my first summer exercise scramble, which also involved the whole Horsham wing. The target turned out to be a stream of B-29s coming in over Yarmouth at 15,000 ft. By the time we saw them we were already at 20,000 ft, and Bertie calmly announced that we would attack them vertically from above. I had never seen or heard of this type of attack before and I didn't know quite what to expect. He rolled his Meteor upside down and fell away below. In order to keep him in sight I was forced to do the same thing, and soon found myself diving absolutely vertically, struggling to keep in touch, while at the same time also observing the rapidly approaching top plan view of a B-29. It appeared that Bertie was determined to fly straight through his chosen target, and I hung on to him grimly, fully throttled back and with airbrakes out. We flashed by only feet behind the tail of the B-29, and then Bertie pulled hard out of the dive and zoom-climbed back to height to immediately do the same thing again. In this way we worked our way along the bomber stream. This was the Meteor in its element, operating against a target that was flying at a speed and height that gave the jet an enormous performance advantage. It was one of the most invigorating and thrilling sorties of my two years on 74 Squadron. Shortly afterwards, Bertie was made an acting squadron leader, and left to become CO of 19 Squadron at Church Fenton.

Later in my squadron tour I was leading a formation scrambled on another summer exercise when we were vectored to attack a convoy passing up the Norfolk coast off Cromer. We found the convoy defended by Fleet Air Arm Sea Furies, and immediately engaged them, becoming involved in very-low-level dogfights over the sea and in among the ships. During one of these dogfights my No. 2 saved my life by yelling 'Red Leader, pull up, too low!' He later explained that he could clearly see my jet-wake on the surface of the sea as I attempted to get good camera-gun footage of the Sea Fury I was following.

Probably as a result of my initial unpopularity with the CO, the Meteor F.8 I was allocated as my 'personal' mount was a real old dog. In fact it carried the identification letter 'D' and was therefore always referred to as D-Dog. It was an early production model, serial VZ512, and lacked the improvements coming through on the newer aircraft such as the larger engine intakes (always referred to as 'deep breathers'), all-clear canopy and spring-tab ailerons. In fact, the geared-tab ailerons on this aircraft were desperately heavy, and much physical effort was required to manoeuvre it. Above 250 knots it became progressively right wing heavy, such that both hands and a knee were required to hold the wing up at 350 knots – the effort that was needed to control that frightful aeroplane when formation flying was immense!

It was this aircraft that gave me one of my biggest frights in a lifetime of flying when the canopy disintegrated with a huge bang at 27,000 ft in the middle of a cross-over turn in battle formation. I was blinded by cockpit dust disturbed by this explosive decompression and had to scratch the ice off the airspeed indicator, compass and altimeter in order to find my way back to base. Luckily the weather was good. Apart from the inconveniences mentioned above, as I was only in a flying-suit over my underwear, I was frozen with cold and soon realised that a bigger worry was that the ejector seat firing blind was flapping wildly, having partially deployed out of its housing on top of the seat. If it really caught the slipstream the seat would fire and the Meteor and I would part company! Needless to say I flew back to Horsham very slowly, and it was a blue-with-cold, but very much relieved, pilot who brought his aircraft to a stop on the runway while an airman climbed up and inserted the ejector seat safety pin. Eventually D-Dog was routinely subjected to a major inspection, during which it was found that the main spar was cracked. That almost certainly explained its weird handling characteristics. It didn't ever reappear on the squadron order of battle and I believe that it was unceremoniously scrapped.

Looking back, I think I can count myself lucky to be alive considering the structural condition of the aircraft on which I was destined to do much of my early squadron flying. However, that sort of thing was not exactly unusual in those days. I was briefed to deliver a Meteor F.8 from West Raynham to Odiham, where it (and I) was to go on static display for the Queen's Review of the Royal Air Force in July 1953. Imagine my joy when, inspecting the Form 700 before signing for this gleaming, freshly painted fighter aircraft, I observed the bold annotation, 'Straight and Level and Gentle Manoeuvres Only – Maximum IAS 250 knots'. I can't remember what was wrong with that one, but it was obviously pretty dire!

CHAPTER 9

Structural Failures

Among the ten million documents held at the National Archives at Kew is one entitled *Meteor Aircraft – Accidents involving Structural Failure in the Air.* Most official files are closed for thirty years, but this particular report, which is dated 1957, was originally scheduled to be withheld from the public until 1 January 2032. Extended closure periods are quite often applied to documents that contain sensitive information, but it is strange, to say the least, to find such a restriction imposed on a report relating to an aircraft that was patently obsolete at the time of writing. The absurdity of this situation was eventually addressed, and this particular file was made available in 2004, although ironically the findings of the many Courts of Inquiry into Meteor structural failures could be inspected at Kew even when the report was still securely locked away. This chapter looks at a number of the accidents that occurred in the immediate post-war years, a time when the RAF was learning the hard way how to operate jet fighters.

In the period 1946–53 a total of twenty-seven Meteors crashed as a result of an in-flight break-up (this total does not include collisions where aircraft subsequently disintegrated). The first occurred on 9 May 1946 and involved Meteor F.4 EE578, which featured long-span wings. It was being flown by Mr Llewellyn Moss of Glosters on a test flight, and having taken off from Moreton Valence it was then seen approaching Defford in a shallow dive at a speed estimated at 450–500 mph. The Meteor then executed a sharp climbing turn from a height of 500 ft, which produced very pronounced wingtip vortices. As the aircraft climbed through 1,500 ft, a structural failure occurred and it broke up, which led to Moss being killed. After a full investigation it was considered that the primary failure had occurred in the elevator horn balances and that this had led to overstressing of the wings in upload.

A similar accident occurred on 5 May 1947 and involved Wg Cdr Harold Bird-Wilson DSO DFC AFC of the Central Fighter Establishment at West Raynham. He had been briefed to intercept four Spitfires that were carrying out dummy attacks on a railway tunnel four miles south of Grantham, and having taken off at 1105 hrs, he sighted the Spitfires fifteen minutes later. Bird-Wilson dived onto one of the Spitfires from 3,000 ft before zoom-climbing back to 2,000 ft prior to carrying out a second simulated attack. He got into position with a left-hand turn, during which he noticed a strong vortex stream from his port wingtip, and went for the lead Spitfire. This was heading in an easterly direction at 300 ft and flying at a speed estimated at 400–450 mph. He did not press home his attack but throttled back slightly and at the same time pulled the aircraft into a forty-five-degree zoom climb.

As he passed through 400 ft Bird-Wilson heard a loud bang, and without any pilot input the control column was pulled hard back and became ineffective. The nose of the Meteor rose high in the air and the aircraft juddered violently as it began to break up. It then rotated in an irregular left-hand corkscrew manoeuvre, at which point the juddering stopped. Using his vast experience, which included having been shot down by Major Adolf Galland during the Battle of Britain, Bird-Wilson quickly jettisoned the canopy and baled out at a height of no more than 1,000 ft. During his descent he saw parts of the aircraft falling to the ground, including the fuel tank, which was hurtling through the air, a blazing mass, to fall about 400 yards ahead of the field in which he eventually landed.

The investigation into the crash concluded that it had been caused by severe overloading of the airframe, resulting in the complete disintegration of the wings and fuselage. The application of the load was considered to have been involuntary, in that the failure of the elevator tips had resulted in a violent up movement of the elevators, with consequent overstressing of the mainplanes. It was recommended that all Meteor aircraft be fitted with strengthened elevators as soon as possible.

A particularly tragic accident occurred on 13 July 1949 when the sole Meteor FR.5, VT347, crashed at Moreton Valence, killing Gloster's acting chief test pilot, Rodney Dryland, who had been heavily involved in the Meteor development programme. VT347 was converted from an F.4 with two vertical cameras mounted in the rear fuselage and further cameras in the nose for oblique photography. The accident occurred as Dryland was descending in a shallow dive but not at abnormally high speed. The break-up sequence commenced with the rear fuselage aft of the transport joint, together with detachment of the tail unit. Both port and starboard mainplanes then failed in download, the remaining structure being destroyed on impact with the ground. It was initially thought that the presence of camera apertures in the rear fuselage might have had some bearing on the accident, but no evidence was found to substantiate this theory. The cause of the crash was then thought to be as a result of failure of the centre-section tank, which had led to a catastrophic break-up of the rear fuselage. However, there was also evidence of premature release of the port undercarriage leg. This was a worrying development as it suggested there were other potential causes of Meteor structural break-ups.

Over the coming months there were a number of cases of buckling to the

Gloster F.9/40 DG204/G was the third prototype and was powered by Metropolitan Vickers F.2 axial-flow turbojets. It is seen here at Gloster's factory at Bentham during engine tests. (*Philip Jarrett*)

osing in front of Gloster F.9/40 DG205/G are (*left to right*) John 'Tiny' Crosby-Warren, Michael aunt, Frank McKenna (Gloster general manager), Frank Whittle and George Carter. (*Philip Jarrett*)

Meteor F.1 EE214/G was used for trials carrying a ventral fuel tank (as seen here), and later flew with 616 Squadron. (*Philip Jarrett*)

One of the first photographs of a Meteor to be released to the press. It was made available for publication on 11 July 1945. (*Philip Jarrett*)

212/G was the third Meteor F.1. (*Philip Jarrett*)

Meteor F.3 of 616 Squadron in an overall white scheme, which was to aid identification.
(*Philip Jarrett*)

A close-up view of an early Meteor, showing the ports for the 20mm Hispano cannon and 'Daunt guards' in the engine intakes. (*Philip Jarrett*)

Meteor F.3 EE247 YQ-B of 616 Squadron. (*Philip Jarrett*)

Meteor F.3 EE317 of 226 OCU. This unit was formed in August 1946 and was formerly 1335 Conversion Unit. (*Philip Jarrett*)

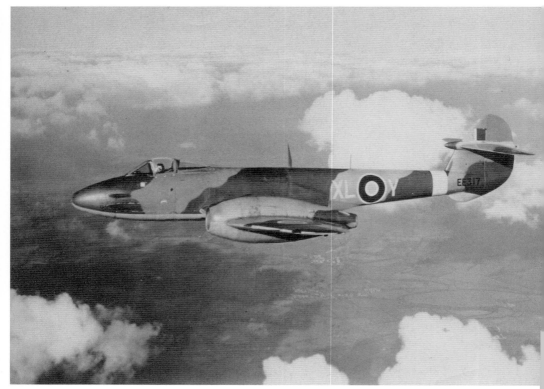

A line-up of Meteor F.3s of 74 Squadron. Note the jet blast marks on the grass behind the aircraft in the foreground. (*Philip Jarrett*)

This view of F.3 EE401 shows to advantage the original long-span wings of the Meteor. (*Philip Jarrett*)

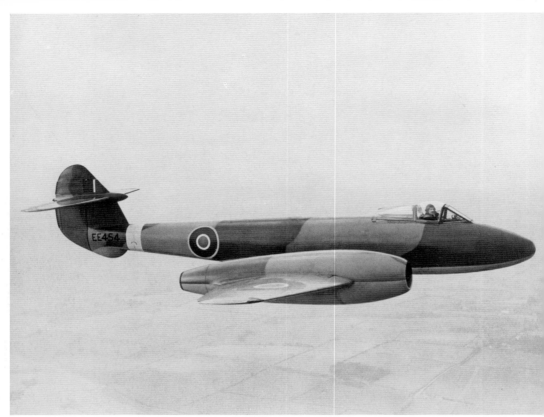

Meteor F.4 EE454 was used by Group Captain H.J. Wilson to capture the World Speed Record at 606mph on 7 November 1945. (*Philip Jarrett*)

During the Speed Record attempt in 1945, Meteor F.4 EE455 featured an all-yellow paint scheme and was flown by Gloster's Eric Greenwood who achieved 603mph. (*Philip Jarrett*)

On 7 September 1946 the Speed Record was raised to 616mph by Group Captain E.M. Donaldson in Meteor F.4 EE549. This aircraft is preserved at the Tangmere Military Aviation Museum. (*Philip Jarrett*)

Meteor F.4 EE519 was used for trials to clear the carriage of underwing drop tanks and bombs. (*Philip Jarrett*)

Photographed in November 1946, F.4 EE592 later served with 205 AFS at Middleton St George. (*Philip Jarrett*)

Meteor F.1 EE227 became the first aircraft in the world to be powered by turboprop engines when i was modified in 1945 to accept Rolls-Royce RB.50 Trent propeller turbines. (*Philip Jarrett*)

The forerunner of the night-fighter variant of the Meteor, F.3 EE348 was the first British jet aircraft to be fitted with AI radar. (*Philip Jarrett*)

Meteor F.4 RA382 was the first of this variant to feature the lengthened fuselage, which went some way in improving directional stability. (*Philip Jarrett*)

The first Meteor T.7 was G-AKPK which was built using the centre section, rear fuselage and outer wings of the F.4 demonstrator G-AIDC. (*Philip Jarrett*)

Meteor F.4s of 203 AFS from Driffield. (*Philip Jarrett*)

Ground crew remove a 20mm Hispano cannon from a Meteor F.4. (*Philip Jarrett*)

The remains of Meteor F.4 VW297 of 205 AFS after it had hit the officers' mess at Middleton St George on 24 November 1951. Pilot Officer R.T. Norman was killed during an attempted single-engine roller landing. (*via Author*)

Another view of VW297, showing the extensive damage to the forward fuselage. (*via Author*)

The front cockpit
of a Meteor T.7.
(*Philip Jarrett*)

A scene that was repeated
many times over in the 1950
This shows a fatal accident t
a Meteor T.7 at Horsham
St Faith in December 1951.
(*Alan Colman*)

Meteor F.8s of 74 Squadron
up from Horsham St Faith
shortly after receiving this
new variant in October 1950
(*Philip Jarrett*)

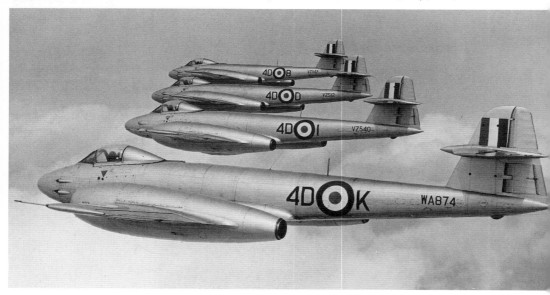

Meteor PR.10 VZ620 on a test flight. The PR.10 was a high-altitude photo-reconnaissance variant that featured the long-span wings and tail unit of early F.4s. It was unarmed. (*Philip Jarrett*)

Top view of a Meteor NF.11 night-fighter. Released to the press in 1951, the caption for this photo describes the Meteor as Britain's 'terror by night'. (*Philip Jarrett*)

G-7-1 (formerly G-AMCJ) was a private-venture ground attack variant of the Meteor. It was famously used by Gloster test pilot Jan Zurakowski for his 'Zurabatic cartwheel' manoeuvre at Farnborough in 1951.
(*Philip Jarrett*)

Meteor F.8 VZ460 was used for bomb and rocket trials by the Gloster company. (*Philip Jarrett*)

aluminium skin of the centre fuselage adjacent to the tank bay when aircraft had been subjected to large positive accelerations with the centre of pressure of the wing in a forward position. This was of particular concern, as distortion or rupture of the centre point of these side-skins affected the rigging of the aircraft by altering the incidence of the wing relative to the tailplane, a situation that was likely to lead to overstressing. Modifications were eventually to be introduced to reinforce this area with a one-piece skin of increased gauge.

During 1950 three more Meteors broke up in the air, and in all three cases it appeared as though overstressing had been caused by the inadvertent lowering of an undercarriage leg. On 29 June 1950, Flt Lt Graham Hulse, who was a flight commander with 'F' Flight of 3 Squadron at the Central Flying School at Little Rissington, became only the second pilot to survive a mid-air structural failure in an early (non-ejector-seat) Meteor. He subsequently recorded his experiences for the Court of Inquiry:

I authorised myself to carry out a practice aerobatic demonstration in Meteor T.7 WA668. I had been detailed to stand in for the Meteor aerobatic display at Farnborough.

After checking and signing the F.700 [the aircraft's servicing and flying records] and completing a satisfactory pre-flight inspection of the aircraft, I took off at approximately 1050 hrs from runway 230 degrees. When airborne I applied my brakes and selected undercarriage up, as the speed was building up to 180 knots. I checked that the undercarriage red warning lights had gone out, before rolling to the left to the inverted position for an inverted climb.

After completing the roll I climbed inverted to approximately 1,500 ft above the ground. During this climb no excessive negative 'g' was applied. At this height I rolled into a steep turn to the left, diving back towards the airfield, where I completed a normal slow roll at about 250 knots.

I then made a wide turn to the north round to the west side of the airfield in preparation for a high-speed run. At 1,000 ft AGL I made a gentle dive towards the airfield and opened up to 14,000 rpm and built up speed to 440 knots over the airfield. This represents a Mach number of below 0.70. This run was made downwind, and weather at the time was nil cloud, perfect visibility, wind 20–25 knots with very little turbulence.

Having crossed the airfield at approximately 50 ft I started a gentle pull-up intending to do a roll off the top. At approximately 600 ft AGL I became aware that something unusual had happened and my immediate impression was that the elevator trim tabs had broken; at this stage the aircraft changed attitude from approximately 30 degrees angle of climb to approximately 70

57

degrees nose up. I pushed the stick forward to counteract this and immediately the nose started to rise, until the stick was fully forward. This had no effect. The loading on the stick was less than normal and the aircraft appeared to be travelling through the air at a very high angle of attack. At this point the aircraft disintegrated with a loud report.

Up to this time I had experienced no excessive 'g', did not black out, nor did I notice any unusual noises – such as would be caused by the lowering of the undercarriage or any yaw or bank whatsoever. At the point of disintegration the canopy blew off and the shoulder straps broke or came off. I found myself being blown back until my head was near the rear instrument panel. My legs were held by the thigh straps. As the speed decreased I was able to get my hand to the straps and released myself. I kicked myself clear and noticed numerous pieces of wreckage about me in the air. I seemed to be well clear, so I pulled my ripcord and a normal descent was made from about 500 ft.

I landed on the grass verge in a small side road near Idbury, and while releasing my parachute harness a car drew up containing two elderly women, and the following conversation ensued:

Woman – 'That was a gruesome sight.'

Myself – 'Yes.'

Woman – 'Are you all right?'

Myself – 'Yes.'

Woman – 'I expect they will be coming to get you.'

Myself – 'Yes, I expect so.'

Whereupon they drove away.

I was picked up some ten minutes later and admitted to sick quarters. Since, I have formed the opinion that the sudden nose-up change in attitude could have been caused by the bending of the fuselage changing the incidence of the tailplane. After the aircraft disintegrated the cockpit section continued in a straight climb, spinning violently to the left.

Wg Cdr Charles Tomalin DFC AFC of the Central Flying School had a good view of the break-up:

I watched the aircraft as its nose began to rise, and at about 400 ft AGL I noticed small pieces falling off. These were followed by two larger pieces and then what appeared to be the whole tail section. A second or so later the rest of the aircraft disintegrated and I got the impression that the mainplanes had broken off. The whole of the wreckage continued along the aircraft's flight path, pieces falling down as they lost momentum, the bulk reaching a height of 2,000–3,000 ft AGL. A few seconds later I saw a parachute descending..Prior to the beginning of the disintegration I saw vapour trails developing beneath the wings. The amount of vapour increased as the disintegration developed.

As a result of this accident and the other two break-ups in 1950, a number of modifications were introduced, which improved the undercarriage mechanism and its associated hydraulic system.

Despite these modifications (1025–1029), accidents continued to occur, and on 17 April 1951 Meteor F.8 VZ527 of 66 Squadron crashed at Linton-on-Ouse. The aircraft was being flown by Sgt B.D. Schnitzler, who had been briefed to carry out aerobatics followed by GCA practice. Weather conditions were excellent with 1/8 cloud at 3,000 ft, a visibility of thirty-five miles and wind of 290/14 knots. Having taken off at 1330 hrs, the Meteor was next seen seven minutes later approaching Linton at 3,000–4,000 ft and doing a roll to the left. After completing this manoeuvre it continued to fly towards the airfield in a fast shallow dive before pulling up into a climb. As it did so, thick vapour trails were seen to come from the wingtips and tailplane, and almost immediately the starboard wing broke off. This was followed by the port wing, tailplane and parts of the fuselage, but as the break-up sequence happened so quickly, the exact order of disintegration, as seen by several witnesses on the ground, could not be established with any degree of certainty.

Once again it appeared as though the overstressing had been as a result of the port undercarriage leg extending in flight due to 'g' loading causing failure of the up-lock. As the aircraft had a full fuel load at the time, with a CG near the aft limit, the nose-up change of trim produced by the undercarriage leg extending at such high speed was enough to cause further 'g' loading, sufficient for the wings to fail in upload. This was the result of the Court of Inquiry. However, further deliberations by the Accident Investigation Branch (AIB) produced evidence that prior to the break-up the port undercarriage up-lock roller was not fully engaged in its hook and that a small positive 'g' loading only was necessary for the undercarriage to be forced from its 'up' position. Although Mods 1025–1029 had been incorporated in VZ527, a further modification (1185) to introduce a redesigned up-lock hook had not been embodied. As a result of this crash it was recommended that Mod 1185 be introduced to all marks of Meteor aircraft as soon as possible and that strict attention be paid to maintenance of the correct adjustment and relation between the up-lock and its engaging roller.

Before the end of 1951, five more aircraft were lost as a result of structural failures, although in one case the pilot had become unconscious due to anoxia and in another the break-up occurred as a result of the hood detaching. On 20 June Sgt J.A. Martin of 66 Squadron took off from Linton-on-Ouse at 1025 hrs in Meteor F.8 WA877 to carry out an aerobatic and GCA practice sortie. Twenty minutes later Mr William Thompson, a farmer from Scalby to the north of Scarborough, heard an aircraft approaching from the south-west and almost immediately after he looked up he saw it break up and fall in pieces to the ground. This particular accident was investigated by John Goulding of the AIB, who once again concluded that it had been caused by the main undercarriage having been thrown from its up-locked position under a high degree of positive 'g'. In each case the respective mounting beams had been torn away with the undercarriage leg. It was noted that the condition of the hydraulic jacks and accompanying up-lock linkages were identical to previous cases, the only difference in this accident being that both mainwheel units appeared to have become extended simultaneously. As this had carried away part of the structure between the fuselage and the engines, it thus allowed structural failure of the mainplane in upload.

One of the worst Meteor structural break-ups occurred on 10 September, as it involved civilian casualties on the ground. Flg Off Lionel Millikin of 263 Squadron took off from Wattisham at 1418 hrs in Meteor F.8 VZ510 for an engine and airframe test, which was to be followed by a QGH procedure. The aircraft's callsign was Handcuff 17, and this was to be its first flight after having had a tank bay skin replacement. Mod 1185 had also been incorporated. The locality for the sortie was not discussed beforehand, but as Millikin was a member of the Southend Aero Club and came from the area it is, perhaps, not surprising that he chose to head in that direction. There was no R/T communication after take-off, but reports were soon received that an aircraft had crashed at Westcliff-on-Sea to the west of Southend.

The last moments of the Meteor were seen by a number of people on the ground. Eric Cole was alerted by the 'scream' of a jet aircraft and saw it emerge from cloud at around 1,000 ft in a 'near vertical dive'. His immediate thought was that it would dive straight into the ground. However, it pulled out, but on completing this manoeuvre it broke up. The Meteor was also seen by R.J. Kniveton-Thorpe, who during the war had been a flight engineer with No. 15 Ferry Pilots' Pool at Hamble. He saw the aircraft approaching from the east in a steep turn to port as the pilot attempted to clear the built-up area. Without any warning, the aircraft 'blew up' and debris fell mainly in Hainault Avenue, Beedell Avenue and Ramuz Drive. Three people on the ground were killed and one was seriously injured.

The Court of Inquiry into this accident found no reason to suspect that the aircraft was out of control up to the time of break-up. It was also thought that the witnesses' estimates of the aircraft's speed had been affected by its low height. There was evidence that the starboard undercarriage leg had forced the outboard door catch and that the tyre had come into contact with the inboard door. Whether this was the primary cause of the structural failure or whether it occurred as a result of stresses set up following another failure could not be established. Of particular concern was the fact that Mod 1185 had been carried out. In view of this it was recommended that consideration be given to testing a Meteor wing to determine the behaviour of the undercarriage and its up-lock under high positive 'g' loading up to the ultimate design load of the wing. At that time nothing was known as to the behaviour of the undercarriage and up-lock above a loading of +6.5 g, and the VG records at RAE showed that, on average, this loading was being exceeded every 200 flying hours.

In 1952 a research programme was undertaken by the Structures Department of RAE in which a full-span F.8 wing was tested to determine its ultimate strength under symmetric pull-out loading conditions. Proof tests made prior to the main test indicated that the maximum load that could be applied to the structure without causing permanent distortions was an acceleration of +9 g. The ultimate strength of the F.8 wing at a weight of 15,250 lb was found to be a load equivalent to a normal acceleration of +11.7 g. The primary failure occurred in the rear spar lower boom in tension at the bolted joint immediately inboard of the starboard engine jet-pipe banjo. As several structural failures in the air showed similar damage, there could be little doubt that in the 'pull-out' case, this was the critical point of the wing. Interestingly, permanent buckling of the centre-section side panels, the most common cause for structural unserviceability on the Meteor, was not reproduced during the tests. After failure of the rear spar, however, with the load redistributed to the front spar, considerable buckling of the side panels was noted. The tests also showed that wing flexure, even at loads equivalent to high accelerations, did not reduce the efficiency of the main undercarriage up-locks, but on the starboard side buckling of the rear bulkhead of the wheel bay had allowed the rear locks of the undercarriage doors to disengage so that the doors dropped slightly at the rear.

There were a total of five Meteor structural break-ups in 1952, the second of which involved T.7 WA665 of No. 205 AFS from Middleton St George, which crashed on 24 April. The aircraft was flown by 30-year-old Flg Off H. Williams, with Flt Lt A.D. Lockyer, an instrument examiner, as check-pilot, and they took off at 0655 hrs. There was a solid overcast at 3,500 ft with tops at 10,000 ft, and visibility was eight miles; however, the flight only lasted just over two minutes as the Meteor was next seen emerging from cloud in a steep dive. It was heading in a southerly direction over Morton Palms to the east of Darlington, and shortly afterwards broke up in the air.

Although tyre marks were found on the inside of the wheel doors, inward buckling indicated that, in this case, neither mainwheel had descended before the aircraft broke up. However, there was diagonal buckling of the tank bay skins, indicating a probable breakdown of the tank bay structure due to excessive 'g'. The Court of Inquiry concluded that the accident was caused by sudden pilot-induced 'g' while travelling fast in a steep dive. With full fuel tanks and an aft CG, the break-up started in the tank bay, resulting in a large, sudden increase in the angle of incidence and a rapid tightening-up in the pull-out from the dive. This theory was supported by one of the ground witnesses, who reported that there was a considerable time lag between the break-up and the impact of the forward fuselage, and that it was his impression that the larger pieces of the aircraft gained height after the break-up, before falling to the ground. This indicated a marked change in the angle of descent (estimated at fifty degrees) which could only have been caused by a significant change in aircraft attitude.

This accident was similar in some respects to the loss of VT347 in which Rodney Dryland had been killed in 1949. By coincidence, Mr J.F. Cuss, the chief stressman at Gloster, had produced a paper the previous month in which he highlighted the initial failure of the riveted joint in the centre-fuselage side-skins, stating that this was the commonest form of aircraft breaking up in the air, as it produced a sudden increase in incidence of the wing under the applied load. Others were not entirely convinced, however, including Mr A.J. Almond of RAE, who pointed out that for this type of failure to occur the aircraft had to be flying at relatively high speed and be subjected to high normal accelerations. In the case of VT347 a large change of attitude would have been needed to bring about the 6–7 g necessary for the tank bay side panels to fail, and this had not been reported by any of the witnesses on the ground.

Although the majority of Meteor structural failures occurred in the UK, some took place abroad, including Meteor FR.9 VZ583 of 208 Squadron, which was lost on 17 June 1952 at El Firdan in Egypt. Plt Off P.J. Poppe was the last member in a battle formation of three aircraft which practised turns as they climbed to 20,000 ft. The Meteors then adopted a loose line-astern formation for a 'tail chase' sequence. The first manoeuvre was a barrel roll, and they then dived to gain speed for a loop. As he went over the top of the loop Poppe checked his airspeed, which was 180–200 knots, but as he appeared to be falling behind he left his throttles open. As he gained speed in the dive his Machmeter was soon reading 0.74, and on levelling out he had the impression of flying through the slipstream of the aircraft immediately in front of him. Almost straight away the starboard wing of his Meteor dropped and the aircraft went sharply onto its back. His recollection of events from this point was extremely hazy, but he thought he heard noises as though the Meteor was breaking-up, and saw a 'circular object' in front of the aircraft which he thought might have been one of the engines.

As there was also no feel or resistance from the control column, he decided to eject, but on pulling the canopy jettison handle, the hood at first did not move, and only released after he pushed against it. On pulling the blind above his head, he was ejected with a 'gentle thump', but did not leave the seat straight away as he considered himself to be falling too quickly. After a few seconds he operated the release box which separated him from the seat, and he then immediately pulled his ripcord. Not long afterwards he made a heavy backwards landing, which injured his spine. As his position and that of the main wreck and the seat marked the points of a twenty-five-yard triangle, it was clear just how lucky he had been.

This accident was investigated by Mr J.H. Lett of the AIB, who was flown out by RAF Transport Command. During his stay in Egypt he sent a letter to Eric Newton, his boss back in the UK, in which he expressed some personal thoughts about the crash. He was not particularly impressed with Plt Off Poppe, and mentioned that this was his third 'affaire' with a Meteor, having baled out of a T.7 in the UK and having written-off an FR.9 shortly after arriving on 208 Squadron, in a heavy landing that collapsed the undercarriage. Lett was also having trouble with the locals, who were keen to purloin as much of the wreckage as they could gets their hands on. Armed personnel were posted to stop this happening, with varying degrees of success. On one particular night they arrested some Arabs and managed to retrieve the material that had been stolen, but as soon as the Arabs were released they realised that one of their Sten guns was missing!

Despite such problems, sufficient wreckage remained for Lett to conclude that the primary failure was the collapse of the centre-section spar structure under conditions of violent up-loading on both wings. The wings had become detached immediately inboard of the engine nacelles, and the tail unit and rear fuselage had broken away as a complete unit at the transport joint. The starboard engine had been thrown clear of the rest of the airframe, which is presumably what Plt Off Poppe had seen before he ejected. Although both main undercarriage units had become detached during the break-up of the centre section, the evidence showed that this had been subsequent to the detachment from the wing and was therefore a secondary effect.

Although most fighter squadrons had, by now, been re-equipped with the Meteor F.8, there was no let-up in the number of structural failures, and in 1953 six F.8s broke up in flight. All of these aircraft were carrying out high-speed manoeuvres at relatively low altitude at the time. Possible factors in these accidents were that the particular high-speed-flight characteristics of the F.8 and its stick force per 'g' could easily lead to embarrassingly high accelerations and stick force reversals. This was discovered during flight testing at A&AEE at Boscombe Down, where it was also noted that there was little difference longitudinally between aircraft fitted with spring-tab ailerons and those with geared-tab ailerons. In a high-speed dive and pull-out there was a pronounced change of trim at speeds above 440 kts IAS, a situation that was likely to be compounded if the aircraft had not been correctly trimmed. On one occasion during testing at Boscombe a Meteor recorded an acceleration of just over 5 g with a pull force on the control column of only 8 lb. As the maximum permissible speed below 2,000 ft was 515 kts IAS, it was clear that there was a potential problem, particularly for less experienced pilots.

The first structural failure of 1953 was not an F.8, however, but another Meteor FR.9 of 208 Squadron, which crashed at Gebel el Ma'aza in the Sinai Desert in Egypt on 5 February. The Meteor (VW368) was engaged in dissimilar air combat training with a Vampire at high altitude when it got into compressibility problems at Mach 0.81. The aircraft entered a steep nose-down spiral at 27,000 ft, and shortly afterwards the control column jerked back and became solid. The pilot (Flg Off P.G. Greensmith) was the subject of considerable 'g', but he eventually ejected safely at 8,000 ft. As he descended on his parachute he saw the tail of the Meteor floating down. It was later concluded that the failure had occurred at around 20,000 ft and had been caused by overstressing in a high Mach number manoeuvre. The next Meteor to crash was WH347, an F.8 from the Central Gunnery School at Leconfield. The break-up occurred at 2,500 ft during a pull-up at around 420 kts IAS, and was witnessed by the pilot of another Meteor. It appeared as though the starboard centre-section leading edge had failed, and that this had led to a general disintegration. The pilot was killed.

The worst time for Meteor structural failures was a six-week period commencing on 18 August 1953. During this period six aircraft crashed, with the loss of all of the pilots (this includes a T.7 that broke up after its pilot was overcome by inhaling fuel vapour). The first to go down was WE964 flown by Flg Off R. Deeley of 66 Squadron, which crashed near Filey. A section of four aircraft was engaged on a tail chase when the No. 4 broke up as it went into a climb. The investigation was inconclusive in this case, as the starboard wing, which had failed first, fell into the sea and was not recovered. The port wing still attached to the centre section fell on land. The accident was nevertheless put down to overstressing during a high-speed rolling pull-out.

The town of Filey was the scene of another crash on 4 September when Meteor F.8 WA778 of 66 Squadron broke up directly over the Butlins Holiday Camp. It was flown by Plt Off B. Whatton, who had taken off from Linton-on-Ouse at 1405 hrs prior to carrying out low flying in a designated area nearby. It was next seen by the pilot of a Meteor F.4 of No. 207 AFS from Full Sutton, who was flying at 1,200 ft. On looking downwards he saw WA778 heading in a southerly direction over the Butlins Camp and travelling at high speed. As it reached the swimming-pool it appeared to bank steeply to starboard, giving the pilot the impression that it was commencing a roll to the right. As it did so there was a burst of flame from the upper wing, which was followed by a stream of white smoke. At that moment it broke up in the air and the wreckage trail extended for approximately half a mile from the Camp boundary. (Although some small pieces of wreckage did fall in the Camp, there were no injuries to civilians on the ground.)

The accident was caused by structural failure of the aircraft during a high-speed 'pull-out' manoeuvre at low level. Inadvertent lowering of the undercarriage was soon ruled out, as the mainwheels were found to have been fully locked in the up position. The primary failure had in fact been in the rear spar bottom boom of the starboard wing due to overstressing. In its report the AIB also felt that a contributory factor might have been excessive speed, in that it was likely that the critical speed of 440 kts IAS had been exceeded. This situation would have been made worse if the aircraft had not been trimmed accurately, as low stick force per 'g' and a vigorous backward pull on the control column might well have produced a disastrously high acceleration. The failure of the wings was typical of overstressing in the positive 'g' sense, and the failure of the rear spar bottom boom was very similar to that of the wing test specimen that had been tested to destruction at RAE in 1952 under symmetrical 'pull-out' conditions.

On 19 September two Meteor F.8s crashed while attending Battle of Britain Air Displays. The first was WA927, which was being flown by Sgt M.W. Warwick of 56 Squadron. Having performed aerobatic displays at Wyton and Cardington, Warwick took off from Wyton to return to his home base at Waterbeach. During his pre-flight inspection he had noticed that three rivets were missing from the middle of the forward lap joint of the starboard tank bay side-skin. He discussed this with ground crews but decided that it was safe to return. However, he stated that he would not risk a high-speed run. In the event he flew over the airfield at a height of 500 ft and an estimated speed of 400–450 knots. He then pulled the Meteor sharply up into a climb so that vortices appeared at the wingtips. Almost immediately the aircraft broke up and parts were strewn along a wreckage trail of about 1,700 yards. Small fires occurred around the main wreckage on impact with the ground. Sgt Warwick was one month away from his 23rd birthday, and was very experienced on the Meteor, with 853 flying-hours in total. His last flying assessment had rated him as 'Exceptional'.

During the Court of Inquiry it was established that Mod 1254, the one-piece 18 SWG tank bay side-skins, had not been embodied on WA927. It was also discovered that two days prior to the accident, a post-flight inspection had revealed that five rivets had pulled on the starboard tank bay side-skin. A repair was carried out the following day after the aircraft had flown several times. Despite this, the evidence indicated that the first point of failure had been the rear spar bottom boom on the port wing at the bolted joint of the spar boom web, an almost identical failure to that identified during the tests carried out at Farnborough the previous year. The sudden transfer of load to the front spar had then caused the front spar boom to fail. The buckling of the tank bay side-skins was also considered to be a secondary effect of the redistribution of load to the front spar.

On the same day, Flg Off P.R. Ward of 74 'Tiger' Squadron was attending the Battle of Britain Display at Coningsby. He took off at 1603 hrs to carry out a low-level flypast before returning to Horsham St Faith. He had been briefed for a level run parallel to the public enclosure and 500 yards out along runway 310. However, he approached in a slight dive of not more than ten degrees along runway 260 at 'moderate' speed and not below the pre-briefed height of 300 ft. After crossing the airfield perimeter he started a slow roll to starboard without lifting the aircraft's nose above the horizon. As the Meteor completed ninety degrees of roll it began to break up. The wings and tail fell slightly downwind of the point of disintegration, and some of these pieces fell among the crowd and in the car park, slightly injuring some of the spectators. The front portion of the fuselage, including the cockpit, came down at the far end of the runway. The engines and fuel tanks went further still, falling 400 yards beyond the airfield boundary.

This accident was investigated by RAE Farnborough, which concluded that the origin of the break-up was severe buckling and tearing of the fuselage centre-section side-skins, which was closely followed by the disintegration of the fuselage and separation of the outer wings. One particularly interesting outcome of this accident was that the buckling was in the reverse direction to previous cases associated with positive accelerations. This suggested that the buckling was caused by the application of negative 'g'. The trajectories of the broken pieces and their location on the wreckage trail showed that the first component to separate from the aircraft was the port undercarriage outer door, and it was considered possible that the inadvertent opening of this door might have been a contributory factor in the application of negative 'g'.

The last aircraft to be lost in this sequence was Meteor F.8 WE856 of 19 Squadron, which crashed at Wolstanton near Newcastle-under-Lyme in Staffordshire on 2 October. Plt Off P.R. Boulton had been authorised for an aerobatic sortie which he chose to carry out near his home. However, his aircraft broke up at a height of about 2,000 ft. The leading edge of the starboard centre section was the first part to be found in the trail of wreckage, and it was thought that the detachment of this might have led to overstressing and structural failure. Sadly, Boulton was killed just a week before he was due to leave the service.

Of all the Meteor structural break-ups thus far, none had been caused by metal fatigue, but this all changed on 13 September 1954. On this day F.8 WE287 of 263 Squadron broke up in the air while turning at about 300 ft during a formation exercise, and its pilot (Flg Off P.J. Derwin) was killed. Its speed at the time was not excessively high at between 320 and 350 knots, and it was estimated that the loading during the turn was in the order of 2 g. The all-up weight at the time of the accident was 15,880 lb. The AIB discovered that both wings failed in upward bending in a symmetrical manner. The primary failure was considered to have been in the starboard side of the centre section through the bolt holes, inboard of the nacelle, of the steel joint plates which formed the lower attachment of the rear spar to the nacelle banjo. The Metallurgy Section at RAE Farnborough revealed that the failure through the bolt holes was initiated by fatigue. This aircraft had flown 935 hours, and records showed that it was the oldest Meteor in terms of flying-hours to break up in the air.

Although Meteors continued to suffer from structural failures in the air, the worst was over, and the modification programmes that had been put in place, together with the use of cockpit 'g' meters and VG recorders, plus a greater awareness by pilots of the flight loadings that were being imposed on their aircraft, led to a significant reduction in the accident rate. This improved situation was also aided by a programme of better education for maintenance crews and better arrangements for the dissemination of data obtained from flight tests for service pilots. Although the accident rate sounds horrific, it has to be set in context, and even in 1953, when a total of eight Meteors broke up in the air, this actually amounted to one every 43,000 flying hours. The accidents involved all marks of Meteor and there was no single cause. At no time did the Meteor lose the affection of its pilots, which shows that they regarded it as a sound, workmanlike design. The problems that were encountered were more to do with its operation and the ingrained attitudes of service personnel, which in the 1950s were still very much rooted in the Second World War. The Meteor taught the RAF how to operate fast jet aircraft, but sadly many gave their lives during that difficult learning process.

CHAPTER 10

Meteor Night-Fighter

In the immediate post-war years the RAF's only night-fighter was the venerable Mosquito NF.36 powered by Rolls-Royce Merlin 113s and equipped with the American-manufactured centimetric-wave AI.10 radar. Although the Mosquito had been a capable performer in the Second World War, it had quickly become obsolescent with the advent of advanced piston-engined bombers, such as the B-29 Superfortress, which cruised at a speed of 300 mph and altitudes of around 35,000 ft. With jet-powered bombers already in advanced stages of development in the USA and UK, the Air Ministry rather belatedly woke up to the fact that Britain's night air defences were inadequate and in need of a complete overhaul. Specification F.44/46 issued in January 1947 was superseded the following year by F.4/48, which ultimately led to the Gloster Javelin, but this was very much a long-term solution, and the problem of what to do in the interim remained. In true British tradition the answer lay in adapting an existing design as a stop-gap measure, but as so often happens, the temporary expedient that resulted was to have a much longer service life than anyone at the time could have envisaged.

The Meteor was an obvious candidate for the night-fighter role, especially a variant based on the two-seat T.7. Trials had already been carried out at the Telecommunications Research Establishment (TRE) at Defford using a Meteor III (EE348) equipped with AI radar, and in October 1946 Gloster submitted a proposal to the Air Ministry for an NF Meteor developed from the T.7. As Gloster was heavily committed with single-seat Meteors, development of the Meteor night-fighter was passed to Armstrong Whitworth Aircraft Ltd at Baginton. Work proceeded quickly under the chief designer, H.R. Watson, and VW413, the fourth production Meteor T.7, was converted as an aerodynamic prototype and flown for the first time with an extended nose on 28 January 1949. Due to its increased weight, the night-fighter version of the Meteor was fitted with long-span wings as used on the Mark III, and all production aircraft featured a tail unit similar to that fitted to the F.8. As the nose was now occupied by the radar (still the antiquated AI.10), the four 20 mm Hispano cannon had to be moved to the wings, immediately outboard of the engines. To increase range, 100-gallon drop tanks could be carried under the outer wings in addition to the normal ventral tank of 180 gallons. The crew had the benefit of cabin pressurisation (a first for the Meteor), the relatively modest 3 lb/sq.in. pressure giving a cabin altitude of 24,000 ft at a true altitude of 40,000 ft. The first Meteor NF.11 prototype was WA546, first flown on 31 May 1950 by Eric Franklin, who was the chief test pilot at Armstrong Whitworth.

As a rework of an existing aircraft, the Meteor night-fighter had few development problems, and it was soon available for test at A&AEE and CFE. WD585 was delivered to CFE at West Raynham on 18 November 1950, fitted with the long-span wings, which featured spring-tab ailerons, AI.10 radar with 'Lucero' facilities (a device for tracking and measuring distance from ground beacons), two TR1934 ten-channel VHF radios, Gee 3, IFF Mk3G and a radio altimeter (AYF). In addition to the cabin pressurisation, electric heating wires were provided in windscreen and quarter panels for demisting and de-icing. First impressions of the cockpit were that the relight buttons were difficult to reach and operate, as they were positioned below the undercarriage and flap levers, as on the Meteor F.4 and T.7 (they were to be repositioned on the HP fuel cocks on later production aircraft). Visibility was inherently bad due to the prominence of both windscreen and canopy framework, a situation made worse by internal icing that was invariably experienced at altitude, despite the de-icing measures mentioned above. As the NF.11 used the same hood as the T.7, it shared the tendency of the latter to occasionally break away during flight. This occurred during the CFE trial, when the hood of WD594 opened in flight and was torn away, luckily without causing injury to the crew.

As the NF.11 was powered by the same Derwent 8 engines as the Meteor F.8, start-up was the same, and idling could be achieved in about thirty-five seconds. Taxiing was simple and the view when on the ground was satisfactory except when the canopy misted up during the landing run following prolonged periods at high altitudes. For take-off at a normal all-up weight (18,300 lb), the aircraft was run up against the brakes and after release accelerated fairly rapidly, although a little more slowly than single-seat Meteors. A pronounced stick movement was required to raise the nosewheel at 90 kts IAS, and the aircraft flew itself off at about 115 kts IAS. At maximum take-off weight of 20,100 lb with ventral tank, drop tanks and a full load of ammunition, the nosewheel lifted at 100 kts IAS and the unstick occurred at about 125 kts IAS. The transition was not quite as clean as at the lighter weight, and the aircraft took longer to reach its safety speed. It was also noticeably heavier on the ailerons. It was found that setting quarter flap tended to improve the take-off characteristics, and in light wind conditions the take-off run was around 1,500 yards.

A considerable number of tactical climbs were carried out in the course of high-speed interceptions, and from wheels rolling, the aircraft climbed to 35,000 ft in just over eleven minutes. Above this height the rate of climb deteriorated, with 40,000 ft being reached in fifteen-and-a-half minutes. With drop tanks fitted the time to 35,000 ft was approximately fourteen minutes, after which the climb rate fell away rapidly. The aircraft would reach 40,000 ft in this condition, but rate of climb and general manoeuvrability were considered operationally unacceptable above 36,000 ft. All climbs were carried out with a full war load. On almost every sortie it became necessary to throttle back slightly at heights above 20,000 ft to prevent surging. Climbs were therefore carried out at 14,500 rpm to 20,000 ft and thereafter at about 14,300 rpm. Surging and associated high jet-pipe temperatures also occurred at altitude if the throttles were opened fully, particularly at low airspeeds. The airspeeds used for climbing were 290 kts IAS at sea level, reducing by 2 knots per 1,000 ft.

Once in the air the NF version of the Meteor proved to be pleasant to fly, with low cockpit noise levels and a lack of vibration. It proved to be quite stable except in conditions of turbulence, when it developed a pronounced snaking, particularly when descending with the airbrakes extended. Although not quite as manoeuvrable as single-seat Meteors, it was more than satisfactory for the night-fighter role. Stick forces at medium speeds were slightly heavier than those in the Meteor F.4, but at greater heights and speeds lateral control was comparable due to the spring-tabs that had been incorporated in the ailerons. The elevators were effective, but greater stick force was required at height, where continuous steep turns and the following of hard evasive action caused a certain amount of pilot fatigue. Rudder control was satisfactory in all respects.

At heights above 35,000 ft the controls all became noticeably less effective. Rate of roll was assessed as moderate, being a little less than that of the Meteor F.8. The maximum rate of turn achieved at 35,000 ft at 420 kts TAS was 360 degrees in approximately one minute ten seconds, although with some loss of speed in the turn. This corresponded to a radius of turn of 1.25 nautical miles. With drop tanks fitted, the aircraft was generally heavier on all controls, with a particular heaviness being noted on the ailerons. Above 30,000 ft manoeuvrability was considerably reduced with drop tanks; there was also a pronounced tendency to wallow in turns, and considerable height could be lost inadvertently. The rate of roll was also a little slower. With drop tanks fitted, the maximum rate of turn at 35,000 ft was 360 degrees in one minute thirty seconds at 410 kts TAS, resulting in a turn radius of 1.6 nautical miles. (Limitations imposed on CFE at the time of test were 5.4 g without tanks, 4.8 g with tanks, and a maximum permitted stick force of 60 lb at speeds above 375 kts TAS.)

In straight and level flight at 35,000 ft, the maximum obtainable speed when carrying drop tanks was Mach 0.74. In all cases the rate of acceleration above Mach 0.70 was slow if a shallow dive was not used to assist in the build-up of speed. Dives were also carried out, and as the aircraft's limiting Mach number was approached (Mach 0.79 above 30,000 ft, clean), a slight nose-up change of trim became evident at about Mach 0.77. With further increase in speed this changed to a progressive left wing and nose-down tendency. No snaking was experienced during these high-speed tests. There were no unpleasant or dangerous characteristics at the stall, the first indications being a certain amount of tail buffeting and a slight pitching and aileron snatch at five to ten knots above stall speed, which occurred at around 105 kts TAS with undercarriage and flaps down and 120 kts TAS clean, depending on the aircraft's attitude. At the actual point of stall the nose dropped gently. For aerobatics the Meteor NF was vice free, and at medium altitude and speed a roll took around six to seven seconds. With drop tanks fitted, the rate of roll was a little slower and the ailerons were noticeably heavier. Loops were straightforward and could be performed without causing excessive 'g'. Generally more effort was required than in single-seat Meteors, so all manoeuvres were performed a little more slowly, but aerobatics were easy and pleasant to perform.

Handling characteristics under asymmetric conditions with one engine shut down were similar to the Meteors previously tested. At climbing power (14,100 rpm) it was possible to maintain directional control until the aircraft was almost stalled, and at this power setting the pilot was able to maintain a speed of approximately 250 knots in level flight. At cruise power (13,500 rpm) no height was lost when flying down to 190–210 kts IAS at 10,000 ft. The critical speed at full power was approximately 140 kts IAS, depending on weight, increasing by around 10 kts IAS when flying with underwing tanks.

When returning at the end of a sortie, deceleration with airbrakes out was considered satisfactory, although not quite as rapid as other marks of Meteor, and there was no noticeable change of trim with the extension of undercarriage or flaps. The biggest criticism during this stage of flight concerned the view out of the cockpit, which was often seriously restricted by ice and/or mist. Also, when flying in rain the forward visibility was virtually nil, and on one occasion during the trial, an experienced pilot made three unsuccessful attempts to land. When he did manage to get down he overshot the runway and finished up forty yards into the overshoot area. There was generally no tendency to float on landing. If the rate of descent was high and a 'round-out' attempted, the aircraft tended to stall heavily onto the runway, so the recommended technique was to make a relatively 'flat' approach to the landing point. Touch-down normally occurred at around 110 kts TAS, and the pilot had to take positive action to hold the nosewheel up until gently lowering it onto the runway at about 85 kts TAS. No difficulty was experienced when landing in a crosswind.

In the case of a baulked landing, an overshoot could be carried out quite easily even when the aircraft had touched down with full flap. Stick forces were relatively light at circuit speeds, and acceleration and climb rate were perfectly adequate. The undercarriage could be retracted rapidly and the flaps could be raised in one movement without trim change. Fuel consumption varied with height from approximately 430 gallons per hour at high altitude to 520 gallons per hour at low level. Safe endurance with a ventral tank fitted (but without drop tanks) was considered to be 0–10,000 ft – 40 minutes; 10,000–25,000 ft – 50 minutes; 25,000–40,000 ft – 60 minutes. These figures allowed for two overshoots on return to base.

As the Meteor NF.11 was fitted with the same AI.10 radar as the Mosquito NF.36, its performance in this respect was no better than its predecessor. The range at which a target could be picked up depended on its type and height, but even when intercepting an aircraft the size of a Washington B.1, the name given to the British version of the B-29 Superfortress, average contact range was only around six to seven nautical miles. Against a Mosquito, pick-up range (at best) was four to five miles, making the navigator's job even harder, given the Meteor's increased speed, which reduced the amount of time available to set up a successful interception. During conventional fighter attacks in daylight pilots found it difficult to avoid the target's slipstream, and it was recommended that the Meteor's line of sight be raised by around one degree so that it was not affected in this way.

As a gun platform, the Meteor NF.11 was stable at all heights in still air, although in turbulence it was prone to snaking, which caused some difficulty in holding a steady aim. Instrument flying could be performed with little difficulty, except when the aircraft was subject to snaking, a tendency which was made worse by the use of airbrakes. At high altitude, and particularly at high speeds, it was found that considerable concentration was needed to fly accurately. This was most marked during practice interceptions when height could be rapidly gained or lost during hard turns. It was considered that recommendations be made for squadron pilots of average experience to restrict the maximum angle of bank to around sixty degrees, as any manoeuvring in excess of this figure was likely to lead to excessive height variations, which could result in an unsuccessful interception.

Although there was no doubt that the Meteor represented a great advance on the Mosquito in the night-fighter role, it was concluded that it was not suitable for the all-weather role due to the fact that it carried no air-interpreted approach aid and was therefore dependent upon GCA and was consequently subject to the same weather limitations as a day-fighter. Any advantage arising from the ability of the navigator to assist the pilot in transferring from instruments to visual flight was nullified by the lack of vision from the rear cockpit. From the point of view of intercepts in cloud it was considered doubtful if the AI.10 radar equipment, with its minimum range of 400 feet, could bring a pilot close enough to the target for him to obtain visual contact. As the NF.11 could not be expected to survive combat with escort fighters, realistically it could only be operated successfully against unescorted bombers above the weather. The most serious drawback of the NF.11 was poor vision created by the design of the canopy and its tendency to become covered internally with mist or ice. Had it not been for the urgent need to re-equip the RAF's night-fighter force, CFE was of the opinion that the Meteor might well have been termed unacceptable for this reason.

The Meteor NF.11 entered service with 29 Squadron at Tangmere with the delivery of WD599 on 20 August 1951. A further seven aircraft had been delivered by the end of the month, and the squadron got ready to carry out intensive flying trials to ascertain if there were any inherent defects likely to affect serviceability. The trial was delayed to the end of November 1951 as aircraft were fitted with direct-vision panels in the windscreens, and the flying that was done in the interim led to the decision to shorten the official trial from 1,000 hours to 500 hours. This was achieved in five weeks at a utilisation rate of fifty-eight hours per aircraft per month. At the end of the period all aircraft were serviceable and there were no accidents or incidents.

Aircraft were operated from the ASP by day and night and were hangared when not in use. The trial was divided up as follows: high-level interceptions (150 hours), low-level interceptions (100 hours), air firing (110 hours), broadcast control (fifty hours), navigation (fifty hours), air tests (forty hours). Around twenty per cent of the total sorties flown reached 30,000 ft or more. Although the trial was completed successfully, many valuable lessons were learned. From a total of 406 sorties, there were sixty-one cases of starting difficulty, comprising fifteen instances of electric failures and forty-six occasions when the torch igniters became fouled. Apart from the length of time taken to remove the top engine cowlings before attending to the igniters, no servicing difficulty was experienced.

In twelve per cent of the practice interceptions flown, the AI radar became unserviceable, which rendered the sortie abortive. The most serious operational deficiency, however, was a very high gun stoppage rate, mostly caused by broken belts and late feeds. A stoppage occurred on seventy-eight per cent of sorties, the actual rate being one in 110 rounds fired. A clean shot was thus virtually impossible, and as much shooting was done with uneven fire power on each wing, there was little chance of hitting a target.

Low-level practice interceptions were made down to a target height of 1,000 ft, with the Meteor slightly below. At this height contact was made at two miles range, but it became much more difficult to identify the target when operating over a rough sea. In this case the navigator's job was made even more difficult due to radar returns from ships and buoys. The range of land-based radars was limited, with many blind areas, which meant that many intercepts had to be flown by dead reckoning. Intercepts were tried down to 100 ft at night, but were found to be impossible. A realistic height for an experienced crew was around 300–400 ft, but even at this height the effect of hitting a target's slipstream was extremely serious and could well lead to loss of control. In contrast, high-level interceptions under Mk3 Gee broadcast control was relatively easy and was considered the best way to intercept a mass raid or a raid comprising ten+ bombers. Gee was also found to be of great value for rapid letdowns to GCA in bad weather.

Although it was only ever intended as an interim solution pending the arrival of the Gloster Javelin, the lengthy gestation period of the latter allowed ample opportunity for the basic Meteor NF.11 airframe to be updated. The NF.13 was a tropicalised version that was produced in small numbers for use in the Middle East. It featured an air-conditioning unit fed by two air intakes just forward of the ventral tank, and the variant also benefited from an improved navigation fit with outer wing aerials for distance-measuring equipment (DME) and a radio compass, the loop aerial being located behind the navigator's position. The NF.13 served with 39 and 219 Squadrons in Egypt, commencing in March 1953. Following the disbandment of the latter, 39 Squadron moved to Luqa in Malta in early 1955 and took part in cover operations from Cyprus during the Suez Crisis the following year. It too was disbanded in 1958.

The much-improved Westinghouse APS-57 radar (British designation AI.21) was incorporated in the Meteor NF.12 to provide a welcome improvement in radar capability. To accommodate the new equipment the Meteor's nose had to be lengthened by a further seventeen inches, raising overall length to 49 ft 11 in. If anything, the extended nose led to an improvement in handling characteristics, although fin area had to be increased slightly to restore directional stability. As loaded weight had risen to 20,380 lb when carrying underwing tanks, more powerful Derwent 9s of 3,800 lb.s.t were fitted. A total of 100 Meteor NF.12s were built, comprising serial batches WS590–639, WS658–700 and WS715–721. The ultimate variant was the NF.14, which finally did away with the poor cockpit view, as it possessed a full-blown hood. Handling was also much improved by the use of a yaw damper, which produced significantly better results during air-to-air firing. Acceleration was marginally better as well, and a well-flown NF.14 was more than a match for a single-seat F.8. The final NF.14 (WS848) rolled off the production line on 26 May 1955, the last of 100 to be built.

CHAPTER 11

Accidents and Incidents

During its long RAF career approximately twenty-five per cent of all Meteors were written off in accidents, which included 150 in 1952 alone. This was not due to any particular problem with the aircraft itself but rather more to the way it was operated. This chapter describes some of the more common Meteor accidents and incidents (all times in the following accounts are 'Zulu' or GMT).

Asymmetric accidents

Throughout this book the first-hand accounts by former Meteor pilots make frequent reference to the difficulties of flying the aircraft on one engine at the lower end of the speed range. The policy of carrying out single-engine approaches to practise for the possibility of losing an engine was to be the biggest killer as far as the Meteor was concerned. Ironically, by the early 1950s the Derwent was an extremely reliable engine and the chances of having to land a Meteor on one engine were relatively low. The following descriptions of landing accidents with one engine throttled back give an idea of the risks involved in operating the Meteor in the engine-out condition.

As an introduction to flight with one engine shut down, training was usually commenced at 5,000 ft with a simulated asymmetric circuit in which the ground was assumed to be 1,000 ft below the aircraft's height. Using a line feature as a 'runway', the aircraft was placed in the downwind position with undercarriage and 1/3 flap down, with one engine throttled back and 12,500 rpm on the other. This exercise was split up into two parts, and during the first part, at the end of the downwind leg, the aircraft was turned through 180 degrees onto the simulated runway with approximately 11,000 rpm on the live engine. At this stage the rate of descent (1,200 ft/min) was pointed out to the student, and at the end of the turn more power was applied. The student was then made aware that the rate of descent had been checked and that with undercarriage and 1/3 flap down an overshoot could be carried out, and by lowering the nose and allowing the speed to build up to 165–170 knots, a rate of climb of approximately 500 ft/min could be maintained. This part of the sequence was usually carried out with the starboard engine throttled back, thus simulating exhaustion of the hydraulic accumulator.

For the second part of the exercise the port engine was throttled back so that hydraulic services were retained, thus allowing the undercarriage and flaps to be retracted as required. Once again the aircraft was positioned on a simulated downwind leg, but on this demonstration the airbrakes were left out. The turn was carried out as before, using 11,000 rpm on the starboard engine, and this manoeuvre was flown at an indicated airspeed of 150 knots. With the airbrakes out, the rate of descent was increased significantly and was usually around 2,000 ft/min, so that 1,000 ft was lost in the first ninety degrees of turn, thereby bringing the aircraft down to assumed ground level. The student was then shown that a progressive increase in power had very little effect in checking the rate of descent and that full power was needed on the live engine; however, even this was barely enough to keep the aircraft in level flight.

By now around 1,500 ft had been lost, and the student was then shown that by removing the drag by retracting the undercarriage, flaps and airbrakes, and by allowing speed to increase to 200 knots, a climb rate of 1,000 ft/min could be maintained. Throughout this part of the exercise, although the foot loads on the rudder were heavy, there was generally no danger of loss of control, assuming that the correct speed of 150 knots was maintained and the aircraft was kept in balance with no slipping or skidding. If any difficulty was experienced in keeping directional control, in most cases a reduction in power on the live engine allowed the pilot to regain control. With undercarriage and flaps retracted and airbrakes in, a power setting of 13,800 rpm on the starboard engine would allow the aircraft to climb away comfortably. As the student had now been shown everything that was likely to happen during asymmetric flight, his training began on actual circuits, with the warning that critical speeds needed to be slightly higher with the reduction of height under actual circuit conditions.

Although, in theory, single-engine flying in the circuit was relatively straightforward, it was easy for a critical situation to develop if the correct speed was not maintained. Each pilot had his own personal 'speed limit', which depended on the amount of force he could exert on the rudder controls. Shorter pilots tended to be at a disadvantage as they lacked the necessary leg length and leverage, requiring them to fly slightly faster than taller pilots. A typical asymmetric accident occurred on 9 November 1953 when Meteor T.7 WL458 of the Central Flying School crashed on Kingham Hill near Little Rissington. It was being flown by Sqn Ldr Richard Fox-Linton and Flt Lt R.G. Mead. Having carried out a simulated asymmetric circuit at 5,000 ft, they made a descent prior to an actual single-engine circuit. Weather conditions were marginal for the exercise but were within limits for the crew. The aircraft was last seen at low level, rolling from side to side in a semi-stalled condition, and it came down on a wooded slope, killing both crew members. On impact the airbrakes were in, although as the exercise involved one circuit with the airbrakes out, it was quite possible that they were only selected in when the aircraft got into difficulties. As both engines were under power when the aircraft came down, it was considered by the Court of Inquiry that a critical speed had been exceeded, with consequent loss of control.

Asymmetric accidents in the circuit were invariably fatal, and another example was the loss of Meteor T.7 WL474 of No. 211 FTS on 1 April 1955, in which Flg Off S.T. Jenkins and Plt Off D.H. Moffat were killed. They had taken off from Worksop at 0923 hrs for a general revision exercise that was to be carried out at the relief landing-ground at Gamston. A roller landing was performed successfully on runway 04 and a high-level circuit was then flown, leading to another roller. Shortly after leaving the end of the runway, the aircraft was seen to yaw to the right and continue in a curved path towards the village of Eaton. The nose of the aircraft wandered to the left and right before the aircraft flicked upside down and dived into the ground. At the time of the crash the Meteor was being flown on one engine, but it was not known if this was intentional or not. From eye-witness reports it appeared that the Meteor climbed to no more than 150 ft above the ground, and the pilot's actions may have been limited by the presence of buildings, including a nearby teacher training college. During the investigation into this accident it was noted that Flg Off Jenkins's critical speed during asymmetric flight at full power was just under 140 knots.

This was not the first Meteor of No. 211 FTS to be lost during practice asymmetric flight as T.7 WL402 had crashed on 4 December 1952 at Lound, three miles north of Retford. At the time it was being flown by Plt Off J.C. Glover and Plt Off D.G. Hopkins, who were examining critical and safety speeds, the effects of engine failure, flame extinction and relight procedure. It had taken off at 1145 hrs, but after a standard R/T call made to ATC ten minutes later, nothing further was heard. At about 1200 hrs, however, two civilians saw the aircraft emit a puff of white smoke at a height estimated to be 1,000 ft. The Meteor then spun one-and-a-half turns, started to recover but then flicked over to starboard and struck the ground, bursting into flames. From the evidence of the wreckage, the aircraft had gone over the vertical before crashing, but the relatively shallow crater showed that its forward speed at the time had been low. It was also established that the undercarriage and flaps were up and the airbrakes were in. The port engine appeared to have been giving considerable power at the time of the crash, rather more than the starboard engine, which had been throttled back. Although it was pure speculation, it was thought that Plt Off Glover may have been demonstrating simulated power failure below safety speed at a height of about 3,000 ft.

Before leaving this type of accident, mention should be made of a crash that occurred at No. 205 AFS at Middleton St George – one that has become the stuff of legend. On 24 November 1951, Flg Off R.T. Norman was flying circuits in Meteor F.4 VW297 on the relatively short runway 28. What happened next was seen by Victor Dabin, who wrote the following for the Cleveland Aviation Society:

> The accident occurred when a Meteor F.4 hit the inside face of the west wing [of the officers' mess] while attempting to perform a roller landing on one engine. I was under jet pilot training at Middleton at the time. I witnessed the accident and was one of the first at the scene. Also, I was interviewed by the subsequent Court of Inquiry as I had flown the aircraft involved just before the prang. It would appear that the accident has developed a bit of a myth status over the years!
>
> The aircraft was being flown by Raymond Norman, who was attempting an asymmetric roller, a manoeuvre impossible for aerodynamic reasons. I was in the crew room in the most westerly hangar when the Meteor went past the window on the ground with full power on one engine. There was just room for a Meteor to pass between the tennis court and a bulk fuel installation, but he managed it. There was one car parked outside the front of the officers' mess – Flg Off Norman's! He still seemed to be trying to get airborne when he hit the car and catapulted into the wing of the mess. The tail broke off and came to rest by the Ladies' Room window. The nose of the aircraft crashed through the wall of the mess and a large lump of masonry fell on the pilot. There were two small explosions as the oxygen bottles fractured. On reflection he may well have been killed by the impact before the masonry fell on him.

Over the years there have been a number of fanciful accounts of this accident, some even suggesting that Norman managed to escape from the cockpit, only to be killed by the falling masonry. On inspecting photographs of the wreckage (reproduced in this book) there are obvious signs of substantial damage to the cockpit area, together with severe deformation of the wing leading edges and engines. Norman died of a fracture to the base of the skull and a broken neck, and it seems highly likely that these injuries were caused by the initial impact and violent deceleration rather than anything that happened afterwards. Among the bizarre coincidences of this accident, as well as hitting his own car, it appears that Norman ended up crashing into his own bedroom in the mess. It has also been suggested that this particular stunt may have been the result of a 'dare', but there is no evidence to support this theory.

After the RAF left Middleton St George in 1964, the aerodrome became Teesside Airport and the old officers' mess was converted into the St George Hotel.

This particular story has endured, as there have been frequent reports of ghostly apparitions at the hotel, particularly in the area where the accident took place. A figure has been seen dressed in lightweight flying-overalls, and many people have reported feeling a heavy, cold pressure on their bodies as they lay in bed at night. It has also been reported that a guest who saw the ghost later painted a portrait of the person he had seen and presented it to the hotel. When this was eventually seen by the parents of Raymond Norman they identified it as being of their son.

Circuit mishaps and the 'Phantom Dive'

Many aircraft were lost in the circuit when the pilot was likely to be under a heavy workload, and if any vital action was missed it could have serious consequences. On 1 May 1951 Flg Off H.M. Taylor and Flt Lt F.A.O. Ralph of the Instrument Training Squadron at West Raynham were returning from an instrument sortie in Meteor T.7 WA678. They flew a QGH procedure followed by two circuits, but when the aircraft was on the downwind leg of the second circuit it was seen to be in difficulties, and soon afterwards it spun into the ground, killing both pilots. It had been airborne for forty-seven minutes, and the small amount of fire at the crash scene gave a clue as to what had happened. Although there was plenty of fuel in the ventral tank, the fuel cock for this was in the off position and the engines had been starved of fuel as the main tanks ran dry. This was backed up by the fuel pumps, both of which showed a degree of overheating, which was likely to have been caused by fuel starvation.

If an aircraft suffered from a technical defect at such low level there was usually insufficient height for the pilot to make a recovery. In the morning of 15 October 1954 six Meteors F.8s of 72 Squadron took off from Church Fenton for high-level practice interceptions. On completion of the exercise they were to carry out a QGH procedure in pairs, the first pair comprising Sqn Ldr T.D. Sanderson and Flg Off J.W. Holland. The former later recorded what happened:

> During the descent at approximately 10,000 ft my R/T No. 1 set failed and I handed over lead of the pair to Flg Off Holland by visual signals and formated on him. He led me back to base on the QGH and levelled out in line with the runway and signalled, 'Dive brakes – In.' I had by then selected channel 'K' on my No. 2 R/T set and heard him call, 'Initials, five miles.' We crossed the airfield boundary at approximately 800 ft, slightly to starboard of the runway. He signalled a break about 400 yards down the runway and broke port to go downwind. I broke almost with him. The break seemed normal at first, but Flg Off Holland's aircraft increased its bank from a steep turn to port until it was inverted, then the nose dropped and the aircraft went into an inverted dive, still rolling to port. This roll continued

until the aircraft was practically upright, and then it struck the ground, where it exploded.

The crash was seen from the ground by Sqn Ldr Edgar Evans:

> I was walking along the tarmac at Church Fenton and noticed two Meteors running in to break. I watched them continuously up to the break, which occurred at an approximate height of 800 ft above the airfield and at a normal speed for the manoeuvre [estimated as 230 kts IAS by Sqn Ldr Sanderson]. To start with, both aircraft broke normally, but the leading aircraft, after turning through approximately 40 degrees in a vertical bank to port, during the first half of which wingtip vortices were noticeable, suddenly rolled quickly onto its back and commenced an inverted dive at an angle of about 30 degrees to the ground. It then completed the last half of the roll in the same direction and then apparently started recovery from the dive, but hit the ground at a shallow angle on the south side of the airfield. It then exploded and burst into flames, the wreckage spreading about 200 yards. By this time I was already running towards the wreckage, which I reached shortly after the ambulance and the fire tender, and assisted the Medical Officer in freeing the body of the pilot from his parachute and flying-kit.

Sqn Ldr Evans was of the opinion that the pilot had been in full control for the first thirty to forty degrees of the turn, but that something had then happened for the turn to be continued to the vertical position. The most obvious possibilities were pilot incapacity or a problem with the aircraft's control system. Sqn Ldr Evans had considerable experience flying the Meteor, and stated that it tended to give plenty of warning by juddering before it flicked into an uncontrollable roll. He could also not recall any other occasion when a Meteor had flicked during a landing break. He was also of the opinion that the aircraft was under control during the roll-out from the inverted position, and considered it to have been an attempted pull-out by the pilot.

The Court of Inquiry agreed that it would have been virtually impossible for the aircraft to have flick-rolled within the first thirty to forty degrees of a turn downwind, but it was also of the opinion that once the aircraft had assumed the inverted position at 800 ft, with the stick already back to maintain a steep turn, the pilot would have had little chance of recovering. The only possible cause was, therefore, a technical failure of some sort. On examination of the wreckage, the AIB concluded that jamming of the aileron control in a port wing down sense at a critical height was the most likely cause of the accident. There were two possibilities that could have produced this situation, both of which had been noted before in Meteor accidents. The first was bending and jamming of the aileron control rods, and the other was jamming of the universal joint at the base of the control column by a foreign object. Due to the extensive crash damage, however, it could not be established which of these eventualities had caused the crash.

Other accidents raised more questions than answers. On 1 February 1955 Plt Off M.J. Turner of No. 4 FTS at Middleton St George took off in Meteor F.4 VT115 for a night navigation exercise, his route being Driffield, Scunthorpe, Church Fenton and Dishforth before returning to base. Having successfully completed his duty, Turner called for a high-level controlled descent from 21,000 ft to Neasham (also known as Croft), which was used by No. 4 FTS as a relief landing-ground. His descent was flown accurately, and the Meteor passed over Neasham at a height of 1,000 ft heading 160 degrees. Less than a minute later it crashed and exploded at Cockleberry Farm to the north-west of the village of North Cowton. It was later reported to have been in a steep side-slipping turn to starboard and diving at an angle of forty-five degrees. Plt Off Turner was killed instantly.

Although there had clearly been loss of control, the reason was uncertain. As Plt Off Turner's flying had given no cause for concern and his R/T had been clear and precise, the effects of anoxia or cockpit fumes were ruled out. In view of the fact that the loss of control had been sudden and complete it was also considered that poor instrument flying was not a factor. Jamming of the controls was also eliminated, as the aircraft flew a straight course after flying over Neasham. It was also noted that failure of the gyro instruments should not have led to such a sudden loss of control. The only unusual circumstance was that the main undercarriage was not locked up. Although it would have been unusual, Plt Off Turner might have lowered the undercarriage on his final approach, but even so he would most likely have raised his wheels again before passing over Neasham. It was thought that the undercarriage might have been lowered inadvertently, possibly in mistake for returning the flap lever to neutral. However, even if this had occurred it should not have been sufficient for the pilot to lose control, unless it was accompanied by another unusual occurrence.

As far as the Meteor was concerned, the biggest danger in the circuit was the 'Phantom Dive', in which directional control was lost when the undercarriage was lowered with the airbrakes out. On 20 April 1953, Plt Off S.B. Ford of 206 AFS took off in Meteor T.7 WG989 from Oakington at 1159 hrs to carry out circuits with roller landings. Three were completed successfully, but on the fourth circuit the aircraft crashed on the downwind leg. From the evidence of eye-witnesses it was apparent that the Meteor had been flying at a height of 300–500 ft and at normal circuit speed. It was then seen to perform a manoeuvre described as a fast, ragged or rapid roll, and was clearly out of control. It was found that the airbrakes were in the out position, the flaps were 1/3 down and the undercarriage was extended about 2/3 down. In an attempt to reproduce the flick-roll that had been witnessed it was decided to fly a test sortie in another T.7 (WG985). The pilots were Flt Lt St John Briggs and Flt Lt A.M. Durrant.

The object of the exercise was to establish whether lowering of the undercarriage with the airbrakes out was an accident risk. Normal downwind conditions were assumed at 1,000 ft, except that the airbrakes were left out. When the undercarriage was lowered the aircraft yawed quite sharply to port and the port wing went down together with the nose. The corrective action taken was that which it was supposed an inexperienced pilot might take, i.e. to attempt to raise the wing with aileron and the nose with elevator. This was completely ineffective, however, the nose continuing to drop and the aircraft to yaw to the left. It was felt that any further increase in backward pressure on the control column would have caused the aircraft to flick. Having lost 300 ft very quickly, the crew wisely felt that it was best to continue the test at altitude.

A simulated right-hand circuit was again flown, but this time at 10,000 ft. The undercarriage was lowered at 175 kts IAS, but where an experienced Meteor pilot would have applied a touch of right rudder, a small amount of left rudder was used as if the aircraft had been over-controlled when straightening out from the right-hand turn onto the downwind leg. Once again the aircraft yawed to port, the port wing dropped and the nose went down. The same corrective action was taken as before, although rather more forcibly, and on this occasion the aircraft flicked rapidly to port through 360 degrees and lost 600–1,000 ft in height. It was considered that had left rudder been kept on the aircraft would have continued into a spin to the left. On the other hand, if harsh right rudder had been applied at the same time as trying to raise the wing and nose with aileron and elevator, it was felt that the aircraft would have straightened out momentarily before flicking to the right. No attempt was made to achieve this, owing to the possibility of structural damage being caused by these flick manoeuvres.

Further trials were flown by Wg Cdr Charles Tomalin DFC AFC, who was the chief flying instructor at No. 206 AFS. His findings were very similar, and when he applied right rudder to counteract the yaw to the left and attempted to raise the nose by pulling back on the control column, the aircraft immediately rolled rapidly to starboard and lost 2,000 ft in height. During this roll the aircraft was completely out of control. As Plt Off Ford was relatively inexperienced and had previously flown piston-engined Harvards, it was felt that he might have had a tendency to use excessive rudder in the early stages of his Meteor flying, having become accustomed to this during his basic training.

The Phantom Dive continued to take lives, and the last Meteor to be lost in an accident was T.7 WF791, which crashed near Coventry Airport during a demonstration on 30 May 1988. This passed off uneventfully until a wingover was attempted to the right to position the aircraft for a flypast along the display line with undercarriage and flaps down. Contrary to normal practice, the sequence had been flown up to this point with the airbrakes extended. As the wingover was commenced, one quarter flap had been extended and the undercarriage was lowered as the Meteor climbed to the high point of the manoeuvre. As it began a descending turn towards the airfield, the bank angle of the aircraft suddenly increased and the nose dropped to about forty-five degrees below the horizon. By this time the wings were level and this nose-down attitude was maintained until shortly before impact with the ground, when a roll to the right was noted. The Meteor crashed in a clear area near the airfield and was completely destroyed. The pilot (Flt Lt Peter Stacey) was killed instantly.

Film taken of the Meteor during the display confirmed that airbrakes had been deployed during the sequence, and it was estimated that its speed at the time of the final dive was of the order of 150 knots. The accident investigation made it clear that all the various criteria for a Phantom Dive were present, and that the accident was the result of an undemanded dive due to the airbrakes being extended at low airspeed. The accident report included the following from the Meteor T.7 Pilot's Notes:

> If the aircraft is yawed at speeds below 170 knots with airbrakes out, the nose may drop suddenly and the elevators become ineffective until the yaw is removed or the airbrakes retracted. The tendency is aggravated if the ventral tank is fitted. Airbrakes should not be used at airspeeds below 170 knots at circuit height and should be in before the undercarriage is lowered.

The turbulence that was produced by the airbrakes at high angles of attack was increased still further by sideslip, and this condition, at a time of marginal directional stability, would result in the loss of elevator and rudder effectiveness and also produce a nose-down pitch. It was also noted that the directional stability of the Meteor T.7 was less than other marks due to its lengthened nose and the size of the canopy. This reduction in stability was reduced even further when a ventral tank was fitted and the nosewheel was extended. Despite the fact that the Phantom Dive had been recognised over three decades before, it had claimed the life of yet another pilot.

LOST CANOPIES

One of the hazards of flying the Meteor, especially the two-seat T.7, was that the canopy was prone to departing in flight, with the risk that it could injure the crew as it flew off, or cause damage to the aircraft. A typical example occurred on 1 May 1951 and involved Meteor T.7 WF786 of 71 Squadron, which crashed twelve miles west of Bielefeld in West Germany. It was being flown by Sgt P.J. Bates, who had SAC P.K. Shanahan (the aircraft's rigger) in the rear seat for air experience. After doing some aerobatics at 10,000–15,000 ft, Sgt Bates decided to finish off with a 'Mach run' at 8,000 ft, in which he attained a speed of 450 knots. He then throttled back and put the airbrakes out, but he felt that the deceleration was particularly violent and was much more rapid than normal. He was about to retract the airbrakes when the canopy blew off.

The aircraft began a sliding turn to starboard which Sgt Bates could not arrest, and so he decided to bale out. However, the release box of his parachute caught on the underside of the windscreen, trapping him half in and half out of the aircraft. By using all of his strength he managed to release himself and went over the port side. He had a fleeting glimpse of the Meteor as he descended, and was aware of some debris in the sky, including one piece which was quite large. He made a safe landing, as did SAC Shanahan. T.7 WF786 was brand-new and was on only its second flight with 71 Squadron.

The accident was investigated by Bertram Morris of the AIB. From the appearance of the hood catches, it appeared as though the hood had not been correctly locked and that it had hinged over onto the starboard side and then been wrenched out from the starboard catches by the slipstream. As the hood produced considerable lift, it probably hinged over until it struck the starboard engine nacelle before breaking up. Marks on the tailplane showed that it had been hit by some of this debris, which caused the rudder to go hard over to port, beyond its normal travel, so that it was wrenched off its hinge brackets. In tearing away, the rudder bowed the elevator control rod and this pulled the elevators hard down. This produced an upload which, coupled with the moment produced by deceleration with the airbrakes out, was sufficient to cause structural failure of the rear fuselage and for the tail section to break away.

Another Meteor T.7 was written off as a result of losing its canopy on 10 April 1952. This was WA636, which was fitted with special instrumentation and was being used by the Institute of Aviation Medicine at RAE Farnborough. The crew comprised Sqn Ldr K. Bazarnik, who was the pilot, with Flg Off A.B. Goorney acting as observer in the rear cockpit. Sqn Ldr Bazarnik later described what happened:

> After two circuits over the aerodrome, during which the compasses and radio altimeter were again checked and my seat adjusted to a comfortable

height for low-level navigation, a run at an altitude of 50 ft was made over the aerodrome on the course of the low-level track (Farnborough–Sidmouth). All the 'operational' instruments were switched on and the observer instructed to commence his observations, i.e. checking times and track position. Apart from slight buffeting due to moderately turbulent air, the aircraft behaved normally.

When the aircraft was reaching 380 knots at approximately 40 ft altitude, about three miles from the aerodrome, there was a terrific bang and a rush of air. The aircraft became unstable horizontally and vertically and was very 'nose heavy'. I immediately closed the throttles, and by pulling the stick fully backwards, and using full tail-heavy trim, I managed to get it out of the dive. Still pitching and rolling, the aircraft veered to the left and I then noticed that the starboard throttle had jammed in the middle position. As I was unable to obtain any reply from my observer, I thought that he might be jamming the throttle by an injured hand or knee.

I then tried to gain height to be able to inspect my observer and the tail unit. I achieved this (about 300 ft) and found the tail unit still there and fluttering, but that the observer was minus his helmet and mask and was slumped forward, his face and hands covered with blood. I therefore immediately decided to land, especially as the aircraft was getting more difficult to handle. By this time I was flying over built-up areas and therefore did not jettison the belly tank. The nearest and most convenient approach was on runway 250.

Struggling with the controls, I managed, partially, to operate the jammed throttle and maintain a speed of from 200–210 knots, which speed produced the minimum instability. On the last leg of the approach speed was reduced to 170 knots and undercarriage and flaps lowered, as I did not want to belly-land on the drop tank. The speed then dropped to 150 knots and I just managed to avoid the hangars when the aircraft started to turn to the right and stalled. On impact the starboard undercarriage failed and the aircraft caught fire. By applying full left brake I just managed to avoid a row of aircraft on the tarmac and the buildings of Flying Control. When stationary, I turned my attention to the observer, but found he was already leaving the aircraft, and I quickly followed.

During the whole time I was airborne I was in R/T communications with Flying Control and gave them a running commentary of the proceedings. On inspection of the aircraft after the crash I noticed that the airbrakes were out. I cannot remember when I put them out and left them there, because all the time I had to operate the airbrakes to regulate the speed, not being able to operate the throttles smoothly.

Although the ventral tank had burst into flames as the Meteor crash-landed, it immediately broke away and the fire did not spread to the main airframe. This preserved the evidence, and it was quickly discovered that the hood's locking-mechanism was out of adjustment between the front and rear cockpits. Even though the pilot had carried out his pre-flight checks correctly and was satisfied that the hood was securely locked, in fact it was not, and once the air loads had built up to a critical value the canopy had released. The Court of Inquiry recommended that servicing personnel be aware of this problem and carry out checks to ensure that the handles in the front and rear cockpits were correctly synchronised.

Another canopy-related accident took place on 7 November 1952, when Meteor T.7 WF823 of 504 Squadron veered off course and crashed on a flight from Wymeswold to Horsham St Faith. It was being flown by Flt Lt W.I. Hart, with Mr C.E. Brown of the Air Ministry in the rear seat, and came down about a mile north-east of Little Bytham in Lincolnshire. There was no R/T call to say that the aircraft was in trouble, but crash investigators soon discovered that the canopy had opened in flight, the main canopy frame remaining attached to the aircraft by the rear locks. The lack of any contact with the pilot suggested that he had been struck by the hood as it broke free and had been rendered unconscious. During the investigation Mr R.C. Clarke of the AIB made the following ominous statement: 'It is a known fact that should the hood open from the port side while in flight, the aircraft becomes quite uncontrollable, and unless the pilot has a considerable altitude, it is more than likely that such an event would have a fatal consequence.'

Problems with the canopy also affected single-seat Meteors, and on 26 October 1953 Flt Lt G.W Hill DFC, who was a flight commander with 263 Squadron, was killed when his Meteor F.8 WH467 crashed at Whitton near Ipswich. Hill was an experienced pilot with 1,500 flying hours in his logbook (including 700 hours on Meteors) and had been awarded the DFC for service in Malaya in 1950. He took off from Wattisham at 1104 hrs with two other Meteors, and not long afterwards took part in the practice interception of a four-engined Washington bomber. Radio contact was then lost, but reports began to come in that an aircraft had crashed in the Castle Hill housing estate to the north of Ipswich. The Meteor was seen by P.C. Charles Frost, who reported that it was spinning to the right and continued to do so until it hit the ground about 400 yards from where he was standing. There were no casualties on the ground.

The crash investigation team quickly ruled out failure of the oxygen system, and it then looked increasingly at the canopy. It was concluded that the hood had detached and had broken its back as it rose at its centre, probably disabling the pilot as it did so. Some of the hood debris, including the rear metal portion, was found over a mile from the main wreckage, which suggested that it had not been jettisoned. It was also considered that the hood might have failed if the Meteor had passed through the Washington's slipstream and that the brief but violent turbulence might have caused the locking-hook to become disengaged.

Another Meteor F.8, this time from 600 (City of London) Squadron, went down on 13 February 1954. Two aircraft, flown by Plt Offs M.J. Bridge and J.R. D'Arcy, took off from Biggin Hill as 'Scroll Red section' and climbed to an altitude of 25,000–30,000 ft for a tail chase exercise. They were seen from the ground by Peter Westcombe, a schoolmaster from Worthing who had been a flight engineer during the Second World War. He saw two vapour trails at approximately 25,000 ft, and looking through a telescope he identified the aircraft as Meteor F.8s. He then observed a large puff of vapour behind one aircraft, which at that time was not making a trail, and shortly afterwards heard a bang. Concentrating on this aircraft, he watched as it maintained a level attitude on an easterly track for approximately fifteen seconds after the puff of vapour. It then began a shallow diving turn to starboard through 180 degrees. The dive then became steeper and the starboard wing went down through about ninety degrees. A violent vertical spin then developed and Westcombe got the impression that the aircraft was out of control. He counted about ten turns of spin before the aircraft passed from his line of sight. A few seconds later he heard a muffled explosion.

The Court of Inquiry into this accident concluded that the puff of vapour that Peter Westcombe had seen was an explosive decompression, as pieces of the canopy landed well short of the main crash site. Among these pieces were the hood metal rear fairing and the hood side-members, together with much Perspex. No other structural failure in the air could be traced. The Meteor flown by Plt Off Bridge (WF754) struck the ground with its airbrakes extended in an inverted dive with the pilot still aboard. He had made no attempt to eject, and it was probable that he had been incapacitated, either by being struck by debris or by the effects of decompression. As Plt Off Bridge had not been wearing a protective helmet, or 'bone dome', which were only just coming into general use, Wg Cdr D.G. Smallwood, the OC of Biggin Hill, was of the opinion that his life might have been saved if he had been wearing one. The Court considered that the hood had become unlocked (the exact reason could not be established) and that the slight opening of the hood had allowed the rear spigots to travel back. The AIB noted that this was the third accident to be investigated in the last twelve months in which the hood had become detached following failure of the locking-mechanism.

IN-FLIGHT FIRES

Although it did not suffer from in-flight fires any more than other contemporary fighter aircraft, this was yet another hazard to the well-being of Meteor pilots, as Sqn Ldr John Miller, the OC of 41 Squadron, discovered on 12 April 1952. He took off from Biggin Hill at 1350 hrs in Meteor F.8 WF700, and was accompanied by Flt Lt R.H.B. Dixon in another Meteor. The two were to have carried out a cine gun exercise at 35,000 ft. Sqn Ldr Miller later described what happened:

> On reaching 15,000 ft I felt an intermittent thumping from my No. 2 engine which was accompanied by a fluctuation in the order of 1,500 rpm. Up to this time the jet-pipe temperature (JPT) and oil pressure had been normal. I pulled back the throttle of the No. 2 engine, levelled out and turned to return to base. In anticipation of asymmetric flight I throttled back No. 1 engine to 13,000 rpm. I was about to shut down No. 2 engine when I noticed that rpm on No. 2 engine had only dropped to 11,800 rpm.
>
> Flt Lt Dixon then called to say that approximately 15 ft of flame was issuing from the starboard jet-pipe. I then noticed reddish-orange flames in front of and in the mouth of the air intake. Flt Lt Dixon then said the mainplane was on fire outboard of the engine nacelle. I decided to eject, and pulled the canopy jettison handle. The canopy came off straight away. While reaching for the jettison handle I noticed No. 2 engine rpm rise to at least 14,700 and JPT reach maximum. A fraction of a second after the canopy had been jettisoned the control column was snatched out of my hand to starboard and the aircraft flicked to starboard in the rolling plane. I reached for the ejection seat fire-handle and pulled the blind down over my face. The ejection seat fired when the aircraft had rolled to starboard through approximately 150 degrees. As soon as I was clear of the aircraft I released my safety harness and found myself free of the seat. I pulled the ripcord and made a normal descent. On reaching the ground I saw I was drifting towards a tree and so spilled the canopy. I was successful in avoiding a landing in the tree but could not prevent myself from colliding with a tree trunk adjacent to a gate post, which broke my fall but at the same time caused minor injuries.

Sqn Ldr Miller landed at Rawreth in Essex and his Meteor crashed at the back of 16 Philmead Road in South Benfleet. The last moments of the Meteor were witnessed by Gordon Johns, who had a very lucky escape as he was in his own garden next door, the crash site being only ten yards from where he was standing. Despite extensive damage, Rolls-Royce was able to establish that the starboard engine had suffered from seizure of the centre bearing, which was a known defect on the Derwent. Failure of this bearing would have accounted for the intermittent thumping and attendant vibration, and it would also have allowed the impellor to foul the compressor casing. Excessive vibration would probably have loosened fuel pipe unions, leading to the severe engine fire that had been experienced.

The following year another Meteor was lost in similar circumstances. On 27 August 1953 four Meteor F.8s of 616 Squadron landed at Wymeswold at 1330 hrs to take part in a 'Rat and Terrier' exercise. At 1411 hrs Ragtime Blue section, comprising Flt Lt Kenneth Brown and Plt Off G. Furness in WE912, took off to operate in the King's Lynn area. They were soon given a target, and both aircraft increased speed, with Furness taking up position behind and below his leader. Not long afterwards, Flt Lt Brown heard a garbled R/T call, which sounded like 'I'm on fire.' He looked round for Plt Off Furness but could see no sign of his No. 2.

On that day PC Alan Atkin was off duty and was standing in his garden in Spalding when he heard a jet aircraft flying towards him at about 2,000 ft. It was gradually losing height and he saw three short smoke trails near the tailplane. When it was nearly overhead he became aware of flames, which appeared to be coming from the centre fuselage. The fire suddenly became much worse, and the flames were of such intensity that they reached the tailplane. A few seconds later there was a small explosion and the canopy flew off. This was followed by a second noise as the pilot ejected. The pilot and seat fell towards the ground, during which time PC Atkin saw him perform three somersaults before he was lost to view. The parachute did not open and Plt Off Furness was killed.

The ejection seat that was fitted to WE912 was a Martin Baker Mark 1E, which had to be operated manually. Plt Off Furness had ejected at 1,500 ft, which was marginal for this type of seat, and he would have had to act quickly to separate himself from the seat and open his parachute. Unfortunately the drogue chute did not deploy, which meant that the seat would have been unstable during its descent, making the pilot's task even more difficult. On examining the ejection seat afterwards, Martin Baker noted that there was no sign of the shear-pin having been fitted to the drogue gun, which would account for the drogue chute not extracting itself correctly. The Court of Inquiry accepted that this was a possible cause of drogue failure (another was a faulty cartridge). however, it considered that it was extremely unlikely that a missing shear-pin would not have been noted during servicing.

Examination of the wreckage established that the starboard engine had been on fire in the air. Although Rolls-Royce examined the remains, the results were inconclusive. Their opinion, however, was that the engine failure was due to excessive overheating in the combustion chambers. The assumption was that there had been over-fuelling due to an undetected fuel leak that had played into the air intake, the bulk of which had then been discharged by the impellor into the combustion assembly.

Another Meteor to be lost to fire in the air was T.7 WA654 of the RAF Flying College at Manby, which crashed on 31 December 1953. It was being flown by Flt Lt R.F. Fisher on an air test, and in the rear seat was SAC Frank Brown, who had been given the opportunity for some air experience. The pair departed Manby at 1420 hrs, but eight minutes later Flt Lt Fisher called ATC to say that he had experienced an engine fire but that it was now out. He requested a priority landing, but a minute later he called again to say that the fire was still there and that he was abandoning the aircraft. After jettisoning the canopy he inverted his aircraft, which allowed SAC Brown to fall clear and descend safely on his parachute. Flt Lt Fisher was faced with a much more difficult task as he was applying a considerable amount of rudder to keep the aircraft straight. As soon as this was released as he attempted to bale out, the aircraft yawed sharply towards the dead engine, and this undoubtedly delayed his exit. It also appeared that his parachute opened before he was clear of the aircraft and became caught on part of the structure. Flt Lt Fisher eventually fell clear, but only a few moments before the aircraft crashed, and he was killed.

Although inverting the aircraft was recommended for the de Havilland Vampire in a bale-out situation, the procedure in a Meteor was for the crew to dive over the side (preferably the port side). If on asymmetric power it was also best to close down the live engine and retrim before leaving, assuming that there was sufficient height available. It was felt that Flt Lt Fisher might have deliberately inverted his aircraft to facilitate the rapid exit of his passenger, accepting the risk to himself. Owing to the advanced state of disintegration of the wreckage, the AIB was not able to establish the cause of the fire, not could it pinpoint which part of the airframe was affected. The crash site was near Louth, about five miles west of the airfield at Manby.

LOSS OF CONTROL IN CLOUD

When one looks at the accident statistics for military aircraft in the 1950s, the words 'dived into ground out of cloud' appear again and again. The increased performance of jet fighters was not matched by any significant improvement in cockpit instrumentation at first, so that extreme care had to be taken when flying in cloud. The early versions of gyro instruments, such as the artificial horizon, had relatively low limits in terms of aircraft attitude before they 'toppled' and began to give completely erroneous information. If a pilot followed instruments that were providing false information it would not be long before his aircraft was heading earthwards at high speed, and in many cases there was insufficient height to pull out when it finally emerged from cloud.

A typical example of this type of accident was the loss of Meteor F.4 VZ410 of 245 Squadron on 13 April 1950. This aircraft was flown by P.II J.A. Brooks, who took off from Horsham St Faith at 1010 hrs with another Meteor piloted by P.II D.J Rhodes. The latter had been briefed to carry out cine gun attacks on P.II Brooks, who was the section leader. Having climbed to 15,000 ft, P.II Rhodes commenced a series of high quarter attacks, but on the fourth of these he flew into cloud as he was breaking away and lost contact with the other Meteor. He called his leader and was told to return to base independently, eventually descending through a gap in the cloud approximately ten miles south of Lowestoft before landing back at Horsham at 1050 hrs. There was no sign of P.II Brooks, and it was not long before reports began to come in that an aircraft had crashed near Darsham in Suffolk.

PC W.D. Martin was on duty on the main road near the railway station at Darsham and heard a roaring noise, followed immediately by three explosions in quick succession. He then saw a column of black smoke rise in the direction of Wolsey House Farm, and noted the time as 1022 hrs. From the last R/T call made by P.II Brooks it was established that the aircraft had lost 15,000 ft in a little under two minutes. The statements of two other witnesses showed that the aircraft had begun to spin after it emerged from cloud. The Court of Inquiry concluded that Brooks had broken cloud in a steep dive and in attempting to pull out had got into a high-speed stall, which had been followed by a spin. Due to the high loading on pull-out, a structural failure had occurred and from the position of the wreckage it appeared as though the primary failure had been in the tail unit. The reason for the pilot breaking cloud at high speed in a dive was not clear, but the two most likely causes were loss of control when flying on instruments or a misreading of the altimeter. At the time of his death P.II Brooks had been with 245 Squadron for eighteen months and had 260 hours on Meteors.

This accident was followed by another eleven days later involving a Meteor F.4 of 226 OCU from Stradishall. At 1512 hrs on 24 April 1950, Plt Off R.W. Jenkins took off in the lead of a section which was to have made a 'snake climb' through cloud to 20,000 ft (the cloud base was 1,800 ft). The participating pilots had been briefed to climb at 280 kts IAS at 14,100 rpm and then turn from 320 degrees onto a course of 090 degrees on reaching 5,000 ft. Plt Off Jenkins made an R/T call to confirm the change of course at 1514 hrs, but a minute later he crashed, having come out of cloud in a high-speed dive. As with many accidents of this nature, there was not a great deal for the accident investigators to go on, although it was clear that there had been another structural failure after the Meteor broke cloud, as both wings had become detached before it hit the ground at Moulton Paddocks near Newmarket.

Although cumulonimbus cloud had been forecast in the area, the other pilots in the section did not report any significant turbulence or icing conditions. Despite this the possibility could not be ruled out that the pitot head had frozen up so that the airspeed indicator had given a false reading. It was also quite possible that the artificial horizon and direction indicator had 'toppled' during the change of course. In the opinion of the Court that was convened to investigate the accident, however, the strongest possibility was that the pilot had lost control of the aircraft through an error of judgement when flying on instruments. It put forward the theory that should the airspeed have been too high at the start of the climb, the pilot might have been tempted to reduce it by easing back on the control column while maintaining the correct throttle settings. The aircraft would have increased its angle of attack steeply so that speed would have begun to fall off rapidly, prompting the pilot to move the stick forward to correct. As he was likely to have been turning to starboard at the time, this action would have brought the aircraft down in a steep diving turn to the right. This possibility fitted with eye-witness reports and the plot of the aircraft's position, but could be no more than just a theory. Plt Off Jenkins was 21 years old and had a total of fifty-two hours' experience on Meteors.

No. 226 OCU was to suffer another fatal accident on 1 April 1952, in which Plt Off M.J. McNair was killed flying Meteor F.4 VZ411. Plt Off McNair had been authorised to carry out an air-to-air firing exercise and had taken off from Stradishall at 1205 hrs prior to meeting up with a Miles Martinet tug aircraft over the Dunwich air firing range, which was just off the coast near Southwold. He was given clearance to begin firing, and the Martinet commenced its tow northwards approximately one mile from the coast at a height of 1,000 ft. After three successful attacks Plt Off McNair was instructed by the Martinet pilot to cease attacking as they were approaching a storm in the Dunwich area. He further advised Plt Off McNair that he should fly through the storm and meet him on the other side. The Meteor was seen flying on a parallel course on the port beam by the drogue operator before the two aircraft entered cloud, but it was next seen flying very low and crossing the coast at Dunwich. Shortly afterwards it crashed into a forest.

It was thought that Plt Off McNair might have been attempting to follow the Martinet visually through the storm and as a result had failed to concentrate on his instruments. The aircraft struck the ground in a dive but the wings were level. It was also noted, however, that quarter attacks had often been known to topple the artificial horizon and direction indicator. Although the height of the tow did not have any bearing on the accident, it was recommended that no firing in future should take place below 2,000 ft.

Another example of this type of accident was the loss of Meteor F.8 WH278 of

616 Squadron on 22 May 1954. This aircraft was flown by Flt Lt H. Blow, who took off from Finningley at 1338 hrs, together with three other Meteors, for an interception exercise. He was the leader of one of the pairs, his No. 2 being Flg Off W.F.B. Willby. After a normal take-off, a climbing turn to the right was commenced at 500 ft, and during this manoeuvre both aircraft entered cloud at around 2,000 ft. The climbing turn was continued, but after a time Flg Off Willby felt his speed dropping off and noted that his airspeed indicator was showing about 210 knots. He then noticed that the rate of turn was beginning to slow up and finally changed to port, by which time his speed was starting to increase again. His altimeter was now reading 5,000–6,000 ft, and it was becoming increasingly difficult for him to keep up with his leader (his ASI was by now increasing rapidly and was passing 350 knots). Shortly afterwards the two aircraft entered some denser cloud and Willby lost contact completely. On checking his instruments again he noted that his vertical speed indicator was showing a maximum rate of descent, he was banking sixty to ninety degrees to port and his altimeter was showing approximately 3,000 ft. When he last saw his leader's aircraft it was in the same attitude as his own and was still flying at high speed. Flg Off Willby corrected his attitude and climbed away, before making a safe landing at Finningley.

The Meteor flown by Flt Lt Blow was next seen by two civilians as it emerged from cloud in a steep dive. It continued on an apparently straight flight path to the ground, where it exploded on impact, killing the pilot. The time of the accident was given as 1341 hrs, or just three minutes after take-off. Flt Lt Blow was an extremely experienced pilot with 1,933 hours' flying-time, of which 593 hours were on Meteors. The accurate description by Flg Off Willby of the manoeuvres that had been carried out in cloud suggested that Flt Lt Blow had been following instruments that were 'running down'. In fact the AIB made the comment that the accident might have been caused by something as simple as a blown fuse. One outcome of the crash was the recommendation that instruments of a type embodying an unmistakable warning device of electrical supply failure be introduced as quickly as possible.

ANOXIA

A number of pilots were killed as a result of anoxia, which could be caused by failure or mismanagement of the oxygen system when flying at high altitude. The effects of anoxia are insidious in that the sufferer is not aware of anything being wrong and, if anything, feels elated and over-confident. However, this feeling is quickly followed by a loss of consciousness. With the arrival of jet fighters, operations were regularly undertaken to altitudes in excess of 30,000 ft, and cases of anoxia became much more common. On 23 August 1951 Sgt S.J. Stewart of 92 Squadron took off in Meteor F.8 WA843 from Linton-on-Ouse at 1515 hrs to take part in a wing formation exercise at 32,000 ft. Sgt Stewart was No. 2 to Sqn Ldr Gordon Conway, the OC of 92 Squadron, and although he remained in formation for thirty minutes at altitude it appeared as though he was out of position on a number of manoeuvres. Towards the end of the exercise he twice called to say that he was suffering from lack of oxygen, but these transmissions were extremely weak and were not picked up by his leader. However, they were heard by Sgt I.H. Panton (White 3), who tried to relay the messages, but he received no reply to his calls.

Shortly afterwards WA843 descended out of control and crashed about one-and-a-half miles north of Catfoss in East Riding of Yorkshire. The aircraft struck the ground in a flat attitude with no forward movement, and the impact caused the ejector seat to fire itself through the canopy, which resulted in multiple injuries and instant death for the pilot. During the descent the rear portion of the fuselage and the tail unit detached from the main part of the airframe at the transport joint, ending up two miles from the bulk of the wreckage. Although anoxia was the most likely cause, this could not be proved conclusively, as a post-crash fire destroyed much of the fuselage forward of the fuel tanks, including the oxygen system. During the Court of Inquiry it was noted that take-off had been delayed by ten minutes, and it was thought that the pilot might have turned his oxygen off at this time and then forgotten to turn it back on again. Assuming that the aircraft's pressurisation system was working correctly, the Court felt that the pilot could have operated his aircraft, although not effectively, for at least thirty minutes at an equivalent altitude of 18,000 ft before finally becoming unconscious due to lack of oxygen. Sgt Stewart had been with 92 Squadron for two years and on his last two annual assessments had been rated as 'above average'.

The highest ranking RAF officer to be killed in a Meteor accident was AVM W.A.D. Brook CB CBE, who was the Air Officer Commanding of 3 Group, Bomber Command. In August 1953 he took a five-day course at the Bomber Command Jet Conversion Flight at Coningsby, and on the final day he was scheduled to carry out an exercise consisting of a climb to 40,000 ft, followed by a high-speed run and a return to base with the aid of a practice controlled descent. AVM Brook took off from Coningsby at 1335 hrs on the 17th, but crashed twenty minutes later. As a maximum rate climb to 40,000 ft would have taken twelve-and-a-half minutes and a descent from that altitude seven-and-a-half minutes, the likely sequence of events was that AVM Brook had achieved his intended altitude but had then succumbed to anoxia. The aircraft then descended almost vertically, in a series of uncontrolled evolutions, but it appeared as though the pilot had made a partial recovery at around 2,000 ft. The Meteor seemed to be under some form of control, although it was apparent that AVM Brook's judgement was still impaired and he might not have been fully aware of his actions. He eventually crashed while flying in a left-hand turn at about 300 knots with both engines at low rpm. As the oxygen system had been set to 'Normal' instead of 'High Flow' as briefed, it was thought that the cockpit pressurisation had failed or that AVM Brook had failed to 'pressurise' before commencing his climb. With 'Normal' flow and pressurisation it was unlikely that he would have been rendered unconscious, even though the oxygen flow was lower than recommended. The fact that he made a partial recovery at low level indicated that there was some oxygen flow at this time.

Throughout the 1950s Meteor aircraft continued to regularly fall from the sky, and another to do so was F.4 VT263 of No. 8 FTS at Driffield on 15 June 1955. On board was 20-year-old Plt Off J.D. Walz of Heidelberg in Germany. He had been briefed by his instructor to climb on a northerly heading at the recommended power setting of 14,100 rpm, and after levelling out at 35,000 ft he was to maintain this setting for a level speed run until his Machmeter was reading Mach 0.70–0.72. He was then to have commenced a gentle descent up to Mach 0.78 and from 20,000 ft was to have carried out a high-level controlled descent down to an altitude of 3,000 ft. He had flown this exercise before with his instructor in a Meteor T.7, but this was to be his first solo attempt.

Plt Off Walz took off at 0946 hrs, and two minutes later he was heard to say, 'Oxygen connected, Angels 20.' At 0954 hrs he obtained a fix from Northern Sector Fixer that placed him approximately over Driffield. Ten minutes later he was seen descending on an easterly heading from the direction of Pickering at a very high speed and at an angle of about twenty degrees. A number of observers on the ground followed the Meteor as it lost height, but none reported any attempt to pull out, and it hit the ground at a shallow angle at Carr House Farm at Cayton, near Scarborough, and bounced into the air before exploding. Plt Off Walz was killed instantly. The aircraft's high speed led to wreckage being spread over a wide area, and although there was no damage to property, some telephone wires and power lines were brought down. Accident investigators were able to establish that the cabin pressurisation was in the forward (pressurised) position and the oxygen was selected 'On'. Despite this, it was felt that anoxia was still the most likely cause, but in this case it could only have been caused by some type of failure in the aircraft system.

COMMUNICATION BREAKDOWN

Although the Meteor could bite if it was mishandled, many pilots were to walk away from potentially hazardous incidents in which they owed their lives to the aircraft's excellent stability and its strength. In the early 1950s Sgt Bob Hillard was flying Vampire FB.5s with 249 Squadron at Deversoir in Egypt. The unit also possessed a pair of Meteor T.7s, and he recalls a lucky escape when flying one of these on a training sortie:

> The Meteors were mostly used for instrument training, and this gave me the opportunity to do a lot of safety pilot work in the front seat. It was during such an exercise that I had reason to be grateful for the stability of the Meteor, and the skill of the ground staff in setting the trim. Sgt Derek Evans was in the back and we set off to do our usual I/F practice, which did not take long to complete. As there was some time left, we let down for some low flying; as a ground attack unit, this was second nature to us, so I had no qualms about letting Derek do this from the back seat. Down went the nose, up went the speed, and as we approached the ground the nose of the aircraft gently rose, eventually settling down to what was probably a good 350 knots, at what seemed like only a few feet above the desert.
>
> There seemed to be some nice smooth flying from Derek as well, but I had an eye on the fuel and suggested to him that it was time to go home. There was a pause, then Derek asked why I was asking HIM to go home. It seemed logical, I told him, as HE was flying it. Another pause. 'But I'm not,' he said, 'I haven't touched a thing for ages.' I gave the pole a little tweak and he was right, there wasn't anyone at the other end. We were both certain that we had done the 'you/I have control' bit, but not a lot was said on the way back.

Another Vampire squadron very nearly lost two of its pilots in a similar incident when flying in a Meteor T.7. Compared with the Vampire, the Meteor was a big aircraft, and some of the junior pilots were rather apprehensive about flying it. On one occasion it was being flown from the front seat with another pilot along for the ride in the back. Their combined experience on type could be counted on the fingers of one hand, and neither was exactly looking forward to the landing. The pilot in the back seat was able to relax to an extent, but as the aircraft began its approach to land his anxiety levels began to rise once again, especially as his colleague appeared to be having difficulty lowering the flaps to the quarter setting, as evidenced by the flap lever continually moving backwards and forwards. Being of a helpful disposition, he got on the intercom and said, 'It's OK, I'll put it down', to which the pilot in command replied with a relieved 'Thank you.'

The Meteor continued its curving approach to the runway and the wings were levelled just before touch-down, but the descent rate was too high and it hit the runway hard before slithering to a halt with pieces of metal flying in all directions.

Both pilots were fortunate to be able to walk away from the stricken aircraft, and it soon became obvious what had happened. When the non-flying pilot had mentioned that he would put 'it' down he meant the flaps, but this had been understood as that he would take over the controls and would carry out the landing. As a result the Meteor ended up landing itself, and the fact that the two were completely unharmed was testimony not only to the aircraft's excellent stability, but to its solid construction.

Imprecise phraseology also led to a near-catastrophe on 19 January 1953, when a No. 205 AFS Meteor T.7 (WA715) was being flown by a student pilot, Sgt P.W. O'Shaughnessy, with Sgt W.H. Black as his instructor. On flying inverted during an aerobatic manoeuvre, a spectacle case emerged from the bowels of the aircraft and struck Black on the head, causing him to offer an expletive. He followed this with a quick 'I've got it', meaning that he had managed to get hold of the offending item, but his student assumed that he had taken control. With no one at the helm the Meteor quickly flicked into a spin, but luckily there was sufficient height to recover. In doing so considerable force had to be applied to the controls, and after landing it became apparent that the Meteor had been over-stressed, and it never flew again.

Aerodrome mishaps

Anyone living close to an RAF aerodrome in the 1950s was guaranteed an exciting time, but as the service continued to suffer high accident rates there was also a certain amount of risk involved. Denis Sharp, who was later to work in the aerospace industry designing power supplies, grew up in the village of Dalton-on-Tees to the south of Darlington. A mere half-mile to the west was Croft aerodrome (also referred to as Neasham), which had been built during the Second World War as a bomber base. Although it fell into disuse after the war, by the early 1950s Croft was being used as a satellite by the Meteors of No. 205 AFS (later No. 4 FTS) at nearby Middleton St George. Denis Sharp recalls two accidents that occurred at this time:

I was born at Dalton-on-Tees in North Yorkshire in 1942, and just after the war finished a Meteor flew low over our house on its way to Croft aerodrome about a mile away. Not long afterwards my father took me to an air display there and I remember Spitfires 'bombing' a cardboard fort. There were also high-speed passes by Meteors which then disappeared vertically upwards. When they landed they taxied over to the crowd. With no health and safety or security worries we were able to have a close look. The Meteor tail pipes were black and smelt of paraffin, and looking down the air intakes everything looked very 'unaerodynamic' with lots of bits in the way. My next encounter with a Meteor was a bit more dramatic.

I went to Croft school from 1947 to 1955 and will never forget one particular day. It was lunchtime and the spotted dick and custard had just been served. We heard the noise of a Meteor's engines getting louder and louder and suddenly there was a large crump. We all leapt onto the tables and looked out of the window. There was a large cloud of grey smoke billowing skywards from the field behind the cookhouse. There had been the stump of a tree at the spot where the Meteor crashed, now there was a smoking crater, just like the one I saw a few years later in the film The Sound Barrier. [This accident occurred on 25 January 1951 and involved Meteor F.4 VW255, which dived into the ground out of cloud, killing Plt Off A.A. McKernan. The aircraft came down only forty yards from a row of houses and narrowly missed two children, Joyce and Kenneth Baker. The pair had watched the Meteor streaming smoke as it came down, and Joyce suffered a minor leg injury and was doused in fuel as it hit the ground.]

From my bedroom window at Dalton-on-Tees I could see the Meteors landing at Croft. The main railway line from Darlington to King's Cross ran past the aerodrome. When they built the railway they had to dig a cutting and piled the spoil in a bank alongside the railway to form what became known as the Spoil Bank, although many locals thought it was called that because it spoilt the view! The Meteors coming in to land had to skim over the Spoil Bank. One day I was playing downstairs when I heard a Meteor on the approach. It sounded different, and then there was a bump and the engines seemed to stop. I ran upstairs and looked out of the window. There was nothing visible at first, but then I noticed a smoky haze near the Spoil Bank, with a man running across a field towards the smoke. I ran down the road to see what had happened, arriving about the same time as an ambulance and a fire engine.

The Meteor had come down about two fields before the Spoil Bank. There was a snapped-off undercarriage leg next to a ditch, and a dead sheep. The Meteor had then gone up over the bank and had then ended up on the railway line. There was no fire or explosion and it was still recognisable as a Meteor. [The aircraft involved in this case was T.7 WL418, which came down on 26 October 1954. It was being flown by Lieutenant Alwan of the Syrian Air Force, who was practising circuits but got too low on his final attempt and struck some trees. He survived the crash-landing, albeit with a severe leg injury. Even after the crash his problems were far from over as he had to be removed from the site by a lorry, since the ambulance that had arrived was unable to get to him due to the boggy nature of the ground. Unfortunately the lorry then ran out of petrol as it was taking him to Darlington Hospital, even though it was only five miles away.]

My last close encounter with a Meteor was when one crash-landed on the aerodrome. It landed on the grass with its wheels up, travelling at right angles to the main runway. To get on the aerodrome was very easy. I just cycled up the road, over the railway bridge, then lifted my cycle over the style and used the path that went to one of the farms. I cycled around the perimeter track, then cut off across the grass to have a look at the Meteor. It had been 'worked on'. The wings outboard of the engines had been removed and laid on the grass. The fuselage centre section was raised up off the ground on trestles and the nose cone had been removed, showing two blocks of metal bolted inside. The fuel tank had been lifted out and laid on the grass – it was about as big as a telephone box laid on its side and seemed to be covered with some reddish brown padded material which I assumed was self-sealing. Thinking back it seems incredible that I could just wander onto a military aerodrome and look at a crashed aeroplane without anyone challenging me.

These were not the only accidents to occur near Croft before it ceased RAF operations in 1955. On 5 May 1953 Meteor T.7 WH246 struck the radio mast as it carried out a low-level pass over the aerodrome. The aircraft became very difficult to control, and the crew (Flt Lt A. Turner and Flg Off K.B. Bones) attempted a forced landing alongside a country road nearby. Unfortunately the left wingtip struck the ground and the tailplane was also damaged. As the Meteor reared up again it flew through a tree and began to break up, one of the engines crashing through the roof of a farm at Great Smeaton. Although no one on the ground was hurt, both pilots were killed.

CHAPTER 12

Meteor QFI

Alan Colman first encountered the Meteor at No. 205 AFS at Middleton St George in 1951, and over the next seven years amassed a total of 1,497 hours on type. He qualified as an instructor at CFS, Little Rissington, in 1954 and later taught at No. 211 AFS, Worksop. In August 1957 he moved, again as an instructor, to the Ferry Training Unit at Benson before converting to the Comet C.2 in Transport Command the following year. Here he describes the Meteor and some of the incidents he experienced during the time that he flew them:

I obtained my 'wings' on the North American Harvard in 1951, and moved onto Meteors at No. 205 AFS at Middleton St George near Darlington. To me the Meteor was just the most marvellous, breathtaking and simple-to-fly aeroplane. Compared with piston-engined machines it was quiet, smooth and incredibly stable, lacking most of the directional and pitch trim changes associated with speed and, particularly, power changes. Perhaps because I had not been flying for long enough to have developed ingrained 'piston' habits, the engine response characteristics were easily mastered – more anticipation was needed initially, not just in making power changes but also because of the weight and sheer aerodynamic 'slipperiness' of the aeroplane, but you soon got used to it. The aeroplane accelerated for ever, and slowed down equally slowly, so there was no desperate need for rapid throttle response.

The landing technique taught for jets was markedly different to that we had had drummed into us on 'pistons' – whereas we had been trained to control the height with the throttle and the speed with elevator, these roles were reversed for jets. Effectively, you pointed your Meteor where you wanted it to go with ample speed in hand, and closed the throttles when you were sure you were going to make it! This change of emphasis removed most of the problems that some of the early jet pilots had found when coming to terms with the change in engine response times. The reserve of power, overall stability and the precision of the flying control response made formation flying an absolute delight – witness the proliferation of formation aerobatic teams formed by numerous RAF units.

The Meteor was the first multi-engined aeroplane I had flown, but as far as I was concerned, I felt that, if she had been strong enough, I could have taught my grandmother asymmetric flying on the Meteor! However, there were a lot of accidents, so it could not have been that simple. The most important thing to bear in mind was SPEED. To control a Meteor with full power on one engine, you had to have strong legs (and the seat position adjusted perfectly) and at least 150 kts IAS. So you never reduced speed below that magic number unless you had plenty of height in hand to convert to speed if you lost an engine. On take-off that was the speed you aimed to achieve as quickly as possible. In addition to demonstrating (at a safe height) the consequences of an engine failure at full throttle and take-off speed (about 120 knots), we used to teach students basic aerobatics on one engine as a means of giving them confidence, and making them familiar with the rule that, as speed was reduced, power on the 'good' engine could only be used with great care and with the resulting yaw perfectly balanced with rudder. Going over the top of an asymmetric loop, for instance, I would demonstrate that it was necessary to almost close the throttle on the live engine momentarily, or control would be lost.

One major trap that the Meteor could spring on the unwary was the effect on asymmetric performance of inadvertently leaving the airbrakes out! Once again I speak from experience, as I had a very lucky escape at Middleton St George, where, on about my third solo in a Meteor F.4, I tried to execute a go-around on one engine, having left the airbrakes out. As I struggled to clear the top of the station headquarters, I fortuitously realised what had gone wrong and whipped them in again. A second longer and I would have been at the bottom of a smoking hole. At that time (1951) there was enormous confidence in the Meteor in Training Command, and asymmetric flying training was regularly performed with an engine completely shut down. Clearly the impact of the rising tide of Meteor asymmetric accidents had not yet made an impact at Staff level, for we were even taught that shutting-down an engine was a marvellous way to eke out fuel if you found yourself running a bit short. On arrival in Fighter Command, however, we encountered a totally different attitude, and I well remember the introductory briefing at the OCU at Stradishall. The lecturer started his address thus: 'In Training Command you will have been taught to shut down an engine if you found yourself getting short of fuel, but you can forget all that. As far as we are concerned here, if you have managed to get yourself into one emergency by getting short of fuel, for Christ's sake don't create another one by shutting down an engine.'

Before the advent of powered flying-controls, the approach to compressibility in anything produced strong trim changes and heavy control forces. The Meteor was no exception. As speed was increased beyond Mach 0.70 the aircraft experienced a strong nose-up change of trim. At Mach 0.80 and above, both hands were required to hold the control column sufficiently far forward to maintain level flight and also to counteract increasingly vicious aileron snatching. Individual aeroplanes had slightly different characteristics – a new F.8 could be ridden to about Mach 0.84, while an old F.4 would have gone out of control at Mach 0.78. In all cases the end came when the control column wedged itself in one or other front corner of the cockpit and the nose dropped. The aircraft would then enter an ever-steepening dive while it flicked laterally from side to side or spiralled. Recovery was straightforward (provided height above cloud or ground was adequate) – close the throttles and extend airbrakes. In due course (usually at about 20,000 ft) the control column would become usable again and the aircraft could be recovered from the dive.

One important difference between the Meteor and some other aircraft of a similar vintage was that the progressive penetration of the compressibility zone in a Meteor produced a naturally self-correcting NOSE UP trim change as speed was increased. I always felt that those types that, early on in the penetration, changed trim nose-down were inherently more dangerous. Critical Mach number (the speed at which the airflow over some part of the airframe becomes supersonic) in a Meteor was around Mach 0.70. While I flew the type there was no specified upper limit – you had reached it when you lost control! However, in its twilight years, a 'Never Exceed Speed' of (I believe) Mach 0.80 was applied to preserve the remaining airframes and reduce the accident rate among pilots who had flown only more modern types that did not exhibit the hairy compressibility characteristics of the Meteor and its contemporaries.

Except as described above, the pitch control forces on the Meteor F.8 were comfortable and matched the speed range of the aircraft, i.e. at high speed they were quite heavy, but then that was what was expected. We did not have 'g' suits, nor was the airframe stressed to the levels common today, so we had no need to be able to apply more sudden 'g' than was necessary (about 4.5 g) to 'black out' the pilot. The Meteor F.4 was not quite as pleasant, as the pitch trim changes associated with changes in speed were more marked, and it was thus difficult to stay 'in trim' during manoeuvres. The aileron control forces were a different story. The F.4 and early F.8s had geared aileron balance tabs. These were acceptable at circuit speed, but became progressively heavier as speed increased so that the achievable rate of roll was seriously impaired above 300 knots, and flying the aircraft at high speed or for aerobatic formation practice could be really hard work. Later aircraft had spring-tab ailerons, which were a vast improvement. Even so, the aileron control on the Meteor was always on the heavy side at high speed, and this did impair its effectiveness as a fighter.

Apart from its heavy aileron controls, the Meteor was a superb aeroplane at low level, being strong, fast and having a good forward field of view. Because of its acceleration and ability to hold speed in manoeuvres, it would (eventually) catch virtually anything once sighted, and could out-climb and out-turn it. At high level, however, it was a different story. The Canberra and B-47 Stratojet were just as fast as the Meteor, but could operate at heights above 35,000 ft where the Meteor was hopeless. At that sort of height, the Canberra in particular could easily out-turn a Meteor and hold its speed in the process.

We had more fun in the 'unofficial' engagements, which were usually against the early model F-86 Sabre. Once again, above 25,000 ft the Sabre was totally superior because all it had to do was take advantage of its greater speed range and dive away. If the Sabres were above you to start with, your only defence was to execute a hard break towards the attack. Each time you carried out such a defensive manoeuvre at height you lost energy and became progressively slower and more vulnerable, while the Sabres (if they knew what they were about) zoom-climbed back above you for another attack. On the other hand, if you managed to find F-86s below you and they were tempted to try and 'mix it', the Meteor could give them a very nasty fright. At 20,000 ft or below, the Meteor could out-turn, out-accelerate and out-climb a Sabre. It also had much more effective airbrakes, which, used at the right time, could cause a high-speed attacker to overshoot his target and become a sitting duck! This was particularly so against the F-86A, which was relatively underpowered and had automatic wing leading-edge slats. In a very hard turn the slats often operated asymmetrically, which caused the Sabre to flick out of the turn. At such a moment spectacular camera gun footage was possible, especially if you had your nose almost up his jet-pipe!

The Derwent was probably the most flexible and rugged jet engine of its day. In the Meteor it suffered terrible abuse but was incredibly reliable. Unlike many other early jet engines, particularly axial engines, it had good surge resistance, and with some care and understanding it could be accelerated to full throttle very quickly. It was possible to get it to surge on occasion – usually when above 25,000 ft – by banging the throttle open from a low power setting when the aircraft was at a very slow forward speed and a high angle of attack. The surge was announced by a series of muffled pops, accompanied by vibration, and the jet-pipe temperature needle jammed at the high end of the scale. Recovery was obtained by completely closing the throttle, then opening up progressively, all the time watching the JPT gauge. I do not remember a Derwent actually flaming out as a result of in-flight abuse, and they never seemed to have been damaged by the disgraceful hammering we gave them.

Our normal operational maximum altitude in the Meteor was usually around 35,000 ft. At that height the aeroplane was at the limit of its performance envelope, and there was a very small reserve of power and speed left for station-keeping adjustments in formation or to engage a target. The highest I ever flew an F.8 was 48,000 ft. I was in a formation of four that had been scrambled to try and intercept another formation of Meteors from the Day Fighter Leaders' School at West Raynham who were returning from a sortie over Holland. The GCI reported that DFLS were at 45,000 ft, so we set out to try and get above them to give us an element of surprise. It was a total farce because, although we did in fact achieve complete surprise, our aeroplanes became totally uncontrollable in compressibility as soon as we began our 'attack', and we passed vertically right through their formation, all of us either upside down or rolling helplessly. In all honesty, the Meteor was virtually useless as an interceptor above 30,000 ft – it was really in its element below 25,000 ft operating against piston-engined targets or jets of a similar vintage to itself.

Until the F.8, all the earlier versions of the Meteor were fitted with flight instruments, mainly suction powered, which had been primarily developed during the latter years of the war. Although the standard RAF blind-flying panel was superb as a concept (and much copied by other air forces), the performance of the individual instruments was not really compatible with the performance of jet aircraft, and many accidents were attributed to this cause. In particular, the take-off acceleration of the Meteor produced a false bank and pitch indication on the suction-powered artificial horizon, which was a killer at night and when entering fog or a low cloudbase immediately after unstick. Similarly, the speed and short endurance of the Meteor required the availability to the pilot of constantly reliable heading information, but before the F.8 it was still necessary to periodically fly straight and level in order to manually update a directional gyro by observation of an old-fashioned 'P-type' magnetic compass.

A further limitation of these very basic gyro instruments was that they 'toppled' (and then gave no worthwhile information for the rest of the flight) whenever any type of 'fighter' manoeuvre was carried out, necessitating much practice of so-called 'limited panel' recoveries to base by utilising basic instruments little better than those fitted to a Tiger Moth! With the arrival of the F.8 came electrically powered gyro instruments of ever-increasing sophistication, with far fewer errors and with the ability for the pilot to 're-erect' them in flight if the much increased 'topple' limits were exceeded. The G4F compass, with sensors in the wingtips to constantly and automatically update the heading information given to the pilot, was, perhaps, the greatest advance of them all, and the harbinger of the rapid developments in electronics which have produced the 'glass cockpits' of today. Later versions of the Meteor T.7 were also fitted with this improved electric instrumentation.

Unlike our foreign counterparts, particularly the Americans, RAF fighters had traditionally carried no navigation instruments at all – recovery to base and location of targets depended on basic pilot navigation skills, augmented by ground radar and ground-based VHF direction-finding services (CRD/F) where these were available. This was acceptable, just, in the UK environment, but posed a serious limitation whenever transit flights or reinforcement involved operations outside it. In about 1953 the first sets of distance measuring equipment (DME) and TACAN (a NATO-standard ground beacon providing bearing information in the cockpit) began to appear in the squadrons – aircraft would appear with these modifications when they returned from major servicing. At last, precision navigation and aircraft to aircraft rendezvous without radar help was possible. Meteors with this equipment sported two small vertical aerials above each wingtip. Apart from the inadequacies of the early instrumentation, the Meteor itself was an excellent instrument-flying platform, with straightforward and progressive changes of trim and great stability. Forward visibility in heavy rain, as in many other aircraft, was always a problem. Some aircraft, particularly the later T.7s, had a suction-powered windscreen wiper. I remember this device more for its temperamental and erratic behaviour than I do for any great efficiency in aiding forward visibility.

During my time on Meteors I did experience a few incidents. As a newly arrived instructor at Worksop I was selected to fly as No. 3 in a four-ship-formation aerobatic team to be led by our even newer squadron boss, who must remain nameless. After a few gentle wingovers to warm up, the leader announced that we were to execute a roll. He began the roll very slowly and without raising the nose perceptibly. By the time we were half-way round we were already diving almost vertically, at which point he realised that he had made a mistake and shouted, 'Break, Break!' Sensing imminent contact with terra firma we all pulled frantically and tried to roll away from the rest of the formation. I saw huge trees rushing towards me and then blacked out. On coming round, shaking, I discovered that my Meteor was climbing vertically through 5,000 ft. There was no sign of the rest of the formation, and I gingerly found my way back to base and landed, convinced that the other three must have died. In fact all of us were all right. The 'boss' apologised, excusing his incompetence on the fact that he hadn't done any formation aerobatics before, except on Bulldogs!

Other incidents included a total hydraulic failure on take-off in an F.8 – I had to pump the undercarriage down and execute a flapless landing after burning-off fuel – and pitot-heat failure that caused the airspeed indicator to freeze, also on an F.8. I had to land using power settings and attitude as I had insufficient fuel remaining to wait for a 'shepherd' aircraft to get airborne. During an aerobatic demonstration flight in a T.7 my seat harness broke during an inverted fly-by, depositing me helpless in the canopy and unable to reach the controls. Luckily another instructor was in the back and he was able to recover the aircraft while I wriggled back into my seat. He thought it was very funny, but I was less than amused.

Two incidents with students come to mind. During a final handling test at Worksop I raised the HP cock to shut down one engine just as we entered the circuit for landing. He responded by raising the HP cock on the other engine. After calling to the tower, 'Downwind on none', I was able to take control and relight one of the engines before we turned finals, making the student complete a single-engined landing. On another occasion the starboard undercarriage leg collapsed during a student landing in a T.7. I was able to take control quickly enough to execute a go-around without anything solid touching the runway. All attempts to lock the leg down failed, and a two-wheel landing was eventually made on the same runway, followed by a graceful curve across the grass as the engine nacelle made contact. No one was hurt and the aircraft was repaired within a week. The cause of the collapse was fatigue failure of the undercarriage downlock, parts of which were recovered from the runway.

Before I arrived at Worksop I took the CFS course for new instructors. Here we practised all the procedures that we would be using when we started to teach our own students. One of the things we used to practise was night circuits with 'roller' landings. One of our number was a well-built, slightly portly individual called Pete Stonham. Pete touched down in his T.7 on one of the night 'rollers' and, as was the procedure, applied full power to go-around without raising the flaps, which were always left fully down until safely airborne and the undercarriage was up. The second he became airborne, with a huge bang, the complete turbine assembly fell off one engine, carved its way through the nacelle and struck the runway in a spectacular cloud of sparks, leaving a groove cut into the concrete. Turbine blades flew everywhere, some penetrating the aircraft's fuel tanks. Now Pete was taken by surprise, an engine failure (in the biggest possible way), well below safety speed and with the undercarriage down and full flap. Being experienced on type, and quick, he snatched enough power off the good engine to maintain directional control, but he would still have died if Little Rissington airfield had not been on top of a hill. To the consternation of those in the control tower, Pete was seen to disappear over the boundary and then sink out of sight into the darkness. However, he managed to use that height to clean up his aeroplane and get enough power on to make a safe circuit and landing a few minutes later – a classic demonstration of the asymmetric handling qualities of the Meteor, aided by brilliant piloting and incredible luck.

I have read in recent years that the 'Phantom Dive' characteristic was associated only with the T.7 and possibly the night-fighter variants, which had a much longer nose and so an increased side area ahead of the centre of gravity. My recollection, however, was that this feature, at least when it was first published, was not mark specific. I seem to remember that warning of the Phantom Dive first appeared in print while I was an instructor on type – around 1955. The warning described the typical Phantom as occurring if excessive yaw was allowed to develop while the airbrakes were extended at low speed. The consequence of this could be an unexpected nose-down pitch and sudden loss of height, which could only be corrected by selecting airbrakes in, removing the yaw and levelling the wings. I do remember that those of us (with the arrogance of youth) who were very experienced on the Meteor regarded it as a situation into which only the foolhardy could get themselves – and felt that anybody who really knew his aeroplane would realise what was happening and correct the situation automatically. Having said that, I do confess to frightening myself thoroughly on one occasion as follows.

Returning to Worksop in an F.8 after a formation aerobatic sortie as No. 2, we ran in, as usual, towards the airfield at low level at 300 knots and in echelon starboard formation. Over the runway threshold, 'Breaking, Breaking, GO' was called and we peeled off at half-second intervals into a very steeply banked climbing turn onto the downwind leg. As one snapped into the break, the throttles were closed and airbrakes extended. Then, as speed decayed through 200 knots one notch of flap was selected (giving a nose-down trim change), followed by undercarriage down at 165 knots and airbrakes in. All this, with lots of practice, would place the aeroplane at 1,000 ft downwind, about 200 yards behind the aircraft in front, with just time to start increasing power and adjusting the trim as the turn continued onto the final approach. It all sounds pretty hairy and very busy, and that is just what it was! On this occasion, however, things went badly wrong for me. When you dumped the gear down in a Meteor the left (port) leg always came down first and caused the aircraft to yaw, momentarily, until the other leg appeared. At this juncture my Meteor, still with around 30 degrees of left bank applied, suddenly headed earthwards. I had time to get the airbrakes in, level the wings and start applying some power, but I was down among the tree tops before I had checked the descent and regained full control. Was that the purist's definition of the Phantom Dive? I honestly don't know, but thereafter, as far as my students were concerned, that was it, I had discovered just how easily you got into it. In the end, that spectacular type of low-level formation break was banned, and as far as I know, it still is.

After his time flying Meteors, Alan Colman was to have a long-term association with the de Havilland Comet, flying the aircraft with RAF Transport Command and also commercially with Dan-Air on leaving the service. He retired in 1991 with a total of 12,595 hours on all types in his logbook.

CHAPTER 13

Spinning the Meteor

During the Meteor's service career the various marks were put through a rigorous series of tests to ascertain the aircraft's spinning characteristics as part of the overall trials programme. These proved that the Meteor was generally reluctant to enter a spin and that its behaviour on recovery was largely predictable. What happened once the spin was stabilised, however, was rather less straightforward.

The Meteor F.4 began its spin trials at Boscombe Down in January 1949, when EE525 was delivered. This was a standard production example except that it featured a parachute installed in the 'acorn' fairing between the vertical and horizontal tail surfaces, and a sideslip indicator mounted on a strut projecting from the leading edge of the starboard wingtip. Spins of up to three turns were made both with and without an empty 175-gallon ventral tank, and were entered from straight stalls or turns. In all cases adequate stall warning was given by buffeting that occurred five to ten knots above the stall. The aircraft showed no tendency to spin at the stall and only entered the spin very slowly, in either direction, when full pro-spin controls were applied. Control forces encountered during the spin and on recovery were generally heavy, but tended to vary considerably. Aileron snatching was severe in many cases, yet hardly noticeable in others, and tended to be worse with the ventral tank fitted. Recovery was usually effected in ½–1½ turns, but the attitude when rotation stopped was usually very steep.

At an all-up weight of 14,810 lb (CG 1.8 in aft of datum, 26.7 per cent SMC), from a straight stall with the control column fully back and full rudder applied, the aircraft yawed slowly through approximately ninety degrees with a small amount of bank. It then rolled over, the nose dropped, and the spin proper began. On one occasion, to initiate a spin to the left, pro-spin aileron had to be applied in addition to full rudder (i.e. the control column had to be moved to the left). The aircraft was equally difficult to spin from turns. Usually it commenced spinning slowly and unevenly in a steep attitude, but the spin became smoother during the second turn, when the rate of rotation was 2½–5 seconds per turn. Total height loss from entering the spin to regaining level flight depended on the height at entry. With a spin commencing at 15,000 ft, height loss was 4,000–5,200 ft, this figure increasing to 5,000–9,000 ft when the spin was started at 30,000 ft. Maximum speed in the recovery dive varied from 190 to 270 kts IAS, and values of normal acceleration varied from 1 to 3½ g. In general, rudder and elevator forces throughout the manoeuvre were heavy, and there was often violent aileron snatching that required two hands to bring under control. These forces were not consistent, however, and tended to vary both during the spin and between different spins.

Spins carried out at an all-up weight of 14,655 lb (CG 3.2 in aft of datum, 27.9 per cent SMC) were generally similar, except that attitude varied considerably for different spins, and in some cases there was pitching accompanied by a fluctuation in the rate of rotation. With a ventral tank fitted, aileron snatching was more severe and control forces appeared to be heavier. Once again recovery was effected readily, but the attitude was steep and if the control column was held too far forward the aircraft pitched rapidly nose down beyond the vertical. The aircraft showed no tendency to re-enter a spin after rotation had stopped.

A further series of spinning trials was carried out in July 1949, and involved Meteor T.7 EE530 (a converted F.4). Despite its lengthened fuselage, the T.7 behaved in similar fashion to the F.4, although it was discovered that some of its less desirable characteristics were exaggerated in spins of over two turns. Once again aileron snatching was apparent and was very violent. For the first two turns it could be restrained by using two hands on the control column, but after the second turn it was impossible to prevent the stick snatching over to the side of the cockpit, in the direction of spin. The force required to centralise the ailerons before moving the control column forward was almost on the limit of the pilot's capability on several occasions. In contrast, the force needed to move the stick forward was only moderate to heavy. There was also intermittent rudder snatching during the spin, and a moderate to heavy foot force was needed to hold on pro-spin rudder, as well as to apply opposite rudder for recovery.

Spins were carried out from 15,000 ft and 30,000 ft, but there was no apparent difference when it came to height of entry or change of configuration (clean/ventral tank). From a straight stall the aircraft entered the spin slowly, first rolling onto its back with the nose dropping well down. Spins to the left were faster and in a steeper attitude than those to the right. Tail buffeting and violent aileron snatching began immediately in the first turn of the spin. At the end of the first turn the attitude became rather less steep, but during the third turn the nose-down attitude increased sharply, and this was accompanied by a considerable increase in the buffeting, aileron snatching and rate of rotation. There was a tendency for the spin to change to a spiral dive after the second turn, in one case the speed rising from 105 kts IAS in the second turn to 155 kts IAS in the third turn. The amount of height lost before regaining level flight varied considerably (4,500–9,000 ft), as did the maximum speed reached in the recovery dive (220–330 kts). These large differences depended mainly on the attitude of the aircraft after rotation stopped. The report concluded that in view of the Meteor's 'unpleasant and dangerous characteristics' it was considered that recovery action should have been completed by the end of the second turn. It was also recommended that pilots should be warned of the aileron snatching and the fact that this behaviour would most likely be worse if spins were allowed to continue beyond two turns.

Bruce Spurr flew over 1,500 hours on Meteors, including two tours as a QFI at No. 104 RFS, Full Sutton, and the Central Flying School at Little Rissington. He recalls the Meteor's stall/spin characteristics:

> Approaching the stall there was buffeting, probably originating from the high-set tailplane, and the nose would drop at the stall itself. Occasionally one wing or the other would drop, but not as violently as, say, the Harvard. In the stall the height loss was rapid, and recovery action, although what one would class as 'normal', needed the fairly rapid opening of the throttles to keep height loss at a minimum. There was adequate warning of an approaching stall, and easing the back pressure on the stick and applying power gave a rapid recovery. With undercarriage and flaps down, or with airbrakes out, the pre-stall buffet was more pronounced.

> The Meteor was not cleared for intentional spinning until about 1954, but normal spin recovery action was usually effective, and spin recovery was added to the training syllabus at CFS and AFS schools. Buffeting was less severe than, for instance, a Spitfire, and the rate of spin would fluctuate according to the pitch of the aircraft – faster as the nose went down, slower as the aircraft pitched up. Considerable amounts of height could be lost quite quickly.

Alan Colman had plenty of opportunities to assess the Meteor's spin characteristics during his time at No. 211 FTS, Worksop, and later at the Ferry Training Unit at Benson:

> As a QFI on the Meteor I was required to train students on all aspects of the stall and spin entry. The normal level stall was innocuous, with heavy pre-stall warning buffet. The nose eventually fell away relatively slowly, and occasionally a wing would drop. The stall in a turn was also preceded by serious buffeting, and nothing nasty would happen unless you kept on hauling, when it would roll either under or over the top, losing height rapidly. Recovery in both cases was easy with a firm reduction in the angle of attack and the wings levelled, while power was progressively applied.

> For the training spin the standard procedure was to climb to around

30,000 ft and then reduce speed in a slight climb with the throttles closed. As soon as aerodynamic buffet was well established (at about 125 knots at that height), full rudder was applied and the control column was hauled fully back. Now most Meteors were reluctant to spin when asked, and it was always amusing to see the various protesting manoeuvres that individual airframes would perform initially, as if trying to talk you out of it! Vigorous yaw and roll was inevitable with the controls held in that position, the airframe buffet was quite violent and it frequently completed two horizontal (shuddering) rolls before the nose dropped towards the vertical and there was a sudden increase in the rate of rotation. At that stage the student was taught to apply full opposite rudder and to push the stick forward, ensuring that the ailerons were kept central. As soon as the rotation ceased, the Meteor, pointing vertically down, accelerated rapidly earthwards, and airbrakes would sometimes be required to limit the airspeed while the aircraft was eased out of the dive.

Other aspects of the Meteor's spinning habits usually only became apparent to those of us who took dogfighting and/or aerobatics seriously! One eventually discovered that pointing vertically upwards with no airspeed at all, particularly at high altitude, could provoke the Meteor to enter a spin of extreme rapidity, which could require an alarming number of turns before recovery action became effective. Occasionally a spin would turn out to be inverted, which, because of the extreme rate of rotation, was almost impossible to spot. In such a case 'normal' recovery action just made things worse, but the aeroplane would recover abruptly if the controls were centralised. I once rode a Mark 8 down from 45,000 ft to 15,000 ft discovering the above!

A comprehensive series of spinning trials was also carried out on the Meteor night-fighter to determine whether the airframe alterations had had any effect on handling characteristics. One of the aircraft tested was WD687, which was put through a rigorous series of spins at A&AEE Boscombe Down in April 1953. This aircraft had begun life as an NF.11, but by the time of test it had been modified to represent the NF.12 with its longer nose. It also featured fin fillets above and below the tailplane 'acorn', which increased fin area by approximately 1 sq.ft. These were incorporated to overcome fin stalling leading to rudder lock at high altitudes, a tendency which had been noted during previous trials. Rudder travel was also restricted to seventeen-and-a-half degrees.

The tests were carried out at a take-off weight of 17,985 lb with CG at 23.2 per cent SMC (1.2 in. forward of datum) with undercarriage up. This position represented the aftmost limitation for satisfactory handling characteristics as determined for the NF.11. A ventral tank was carried, but no underwing tanks were fitted. Trials were carried out at 15,000 ft and 35,000 ft, with two-turn spins being made in either direction from straight stalls and from stalls in turning flight, airbrakes in. Check-spins were also made with the airbrakes extended.

In a spin from a straight stall at 15,000 ft, slight buffet was experienced at 120 kts IAS, together with aileron snatch. The aircraft then made a slow half-roll before dropping its nose into what proved to be a rather erratic spin. During the second turn the rate of rotation decreased markedly and then increased again. On entering the spin, the control column snatched over to starboard, but thereafter about a 40 lb pro-spin force persisted for the rest of the spin (pro-spin denotes a tendency for the control column to move towards the centre of the spin). During the spin only light buffet was apparent. When recovery action was initiated the aircraft responded immediately, although care had to be taken during the pull-out to avoid a high-speed stall. Spins to starboard were similar; however, less variation in the rate of rotation was noted, and there were small oscillations in pitch and yaw. Aileron snatching occurred again, but in this case it was liable to snatch either way, and the aileron force that had to be applied to counteract this tendency was only moderate (less than 20 lb). Spins to port and starboard from turning flight were very similar to those carried out from straight stalls.

In spins to port from 35,000 ft, slight buffet was felt at 130 kts IAS, increasing in severity down to the stall, which occurred at 120 kts IAS. The aircraft then made a quarter-roll and dropped its nose into a spin. The first turn was quite fast, due to the fact that the aircraft had not settled fully into the spin at this stage, but the second turn was much slower and fairly smooth. Aileron forces were moderate, snatching either way, but predominantly pro-spin. Once again, the recovery commenced as soon as opposite rudder was applied and the control column was eased forward. Spins to starboard were very similar, although the aircraft momentarily tried to spin the other way. A slight difference was noted on recovery, as on applying opposite rudder the rate of rotation decreased, before increasing again when the stick was pushed forward. Thereafter the spin stopped almost immediately.

When the aircraft was spun after stalling from turning flight, slight buffet was experienced at speeds as high as 145 kts IAS, and aileron snatch was still present. During spins to starboard the aircraft again showed a tendency to flick out of the turn. In both instances attitude on recovery was very steep, and great care had to be taken to ease the control column back gently to avoid a high-speed stall. Check-spins with airbrakes out showed marked buffet at 125 kts IAS, and the spin was more erratic. During spins to port, aileron snatching was much more severe, particularly during the second turn, and two hands were needed to hold the control column central. This action had to be maintained during recovery, although response was still immediate. Care had to be taken in the pull-out to prevent excessive judder. When spinning to starboard with airbrakes extended, aileron snatching was not as bad, and the aircraft could be controlled with one hand. A heavy pro-spin force was apparent during recovery, the latter commencing as soon as anti-spin controls were applied. In general, A&AEE considered that the spinning characteristics of the NF.12 were satisfactory, and it recommended that the aircraft be cleared for recovery from incipient spins in service.

CHAPTER 14

Pilot Debrief (1)

Despite the fact that it was obsolescent even by the early 1950s and was to suffer a relatively high accident rate, the Meteor was liked by the vast majority of its pilots. It proved to be rugged and dependable and did not have any particular vices if flown by the book. Many of the losses that occurred could not be attributed to any adverse handling characteristic or design deficiency; instead, rather too many accidents were caused by the way the aircraft was operated. Gradually, as experience was gained and attitudes changed, accident rates fell to more acceptable levels, but it was a slow process and the subject of accident rates was discussed in the House of Commons in 1952. Regarding the losses of fighter aircraft in general, Prime Minister Winston Churchill made enquiries and produced figures to show that the chances of a fighter pilot being killed during an eighteen-month tour were one in sixteen. In response, the Ministry reported that such figures were not abnormal and there was no cause for alarm! F. Eastman recalls some of the perils that awaited students at Advanced Flying Schools, and a selection of his experiences with 257 Squadron:

My instructor at No. 207 AFS, Full Sutton, was Sgt Bruce Spurr. On my first trip for familiarisation, Bruce held the aircraft down after take-off and then pulled up into a loop with a half-roll off the top – very impressive, although I believe some students immediately chickened out after this demo! On one of my early solos I was idly looking around the circuit when on the 'dead side', and watching a T.7 taking off, when it suddenly veered hard to starboard and burst into flames. It was on a single-engined training detail, and both instructor and pupil were killed.

Concerning Meteor asymmetric training, on the AFS course one had to do a solo detail of several circuits wherein an engine was closed to idle, a roller landing made, then trim rapidly zeroed, both engines throttled up and round again. For the last circuit one engine had to be completely closed down for landing. Unfortunately this is what killed many people, for not enough attention was paid to the difference that even a small amount of thrust from an idling engine made, compared to a dead one. With the benefit of some forty years' experience, I realise how lucky most of us were, for below about 125 knots an engine failure would have been disastrous on take-off. I must have flown about 1,200 hours on the Meteor, with rarely an incident and certainly never any engine problems, which says something for the Derwent, especially considering the abuse to which it could be subjected. An example is the JPT gauges, which were arranged so that the temperature for each engine shared one gauge, the scale being through about 120 degrees; for the port engine from about the 8 o'clock position to 12 o'clock (12 o'clock being the maximum), and the starboard from about 4 o'clock anti-clockwise to the noon position. However, when tail chasing or dogfighting with coarse power control movements, it was possible to overboost the engine so that the needle for each engine could overlap onto the scale for the other, giving the impression that the JPT was actually reducing!

Full Sutton had two runways, and on one particular day (probably due to a crosswind) an instructor and pupil in a Meteor T.7 were approaching the shorter runway, the approach to this runway being crossed by the railway line from York to Selby, the line running roughly parallel to the main runway and on an embankment. For some reason the aircraft was allowed to get into a low and slow configuration just as a fish goods train was crossing the approach path, and the Meteor finished up gently resting between two trucks laden with fish. Neither crew member was injured, apart from having to wait ages to be dug out of piles of smelly fish!

On 257 Squadron at Wattisham, every new pilot usually got lumbered with the worst aircraft to fly. Plt Off Nick Carter was one of those, and we were tail chasing one day in a four when Nick's aircraft hit compressibility and started flicking out of control. The rest of us, in less bent machines, were OK. Nick didn't realise that if he had left everything alone after the Mach number dropped at a slightly lower altitude he would have been all right. Instead he ejected, or tried to. As we were doing 'cine' in the tail chase, Nick's gunsight was up; unfortunately, when he jettisoned the hood, the gunsight failed to automatically retract downwards. He then hit the black and yellow emergency punch button, but it still did not retract, and with the sight still up there was a good chance of kneecap damage on ejection. He then tried to pull the 'Jesus Christ' blind, but the slipstream pulled his arm out; when he got it back in it was broken (by now, of course, I doubt if he could have flown the aircraft anyway!), so he crept up his face with his left hand and managed to pull the blind and eject, eventually coming to rest in a dirty Suffolk field somewhere near Bentwaters. (This incident occurred on 21 December 1954, and involved F.8 WH299.)

We had another pilot at Wattisham (Sgt Mick Foster) who got into trouble in an F.8 which he was flying on its first flight after a major overhaul. His girlfriend lived nearby, and at about 1,000 feet he did a slow roll over her house. Unfortunately the armourers hadn't secured the ejector seat properly, so as the aircraft became inverted the seat slid up the rails due to gravity and the drogue gun went off. The seat was then firmly entrenched at the top of the rails, so Mick could no longer reach the controls, and with the aircraft now going downwards inverted, he pulled the blind and went the rest of the way. Luckily, apart from some bruises, he was uninjured. At the subsequent Court of Inquiry the observation was made that he should have first attempted to regain control by trying to reach the seat-pan adjustment handle. They seriously thought that it would be possible to raise what was now an inverted hot-seat in an inverted aeroplane against the forces of gravity and the weight of the seat! We all felt that this was a terrible criticism and showed how out of touch many Staff people were with the real world.

In the immediate post war period some RAF stations had a reputation for continuing to operate in extremely marginal weather conditions. Bob Hillard recalls such an occasion when he was training at No. 203 AFS at Driffield:

One particular flight on 15 November 1949 nearly brought disaster. The met forecast at briefing suggested possible fog moving in, but with the prevailing mood at No. 203 AFS, particularly that of one individual, it was unlikely that flying would be suspended for the time being, and that turned out to be the case. PII Reg Willis was my instructor for the planned exercise of upper air work, followed by some medium-altitude manoeuvring. The checks were carried out with blue skies above but grey ahead, and then it was off to the runway with a final brake check to 11,000 revs before take-off. Brakes off and we accelerated rapidly down the runway, over the boundary and into fog! I remember going onto instruments, and a check on the artificial horizon showed a nose-up situation. I also remember the sight of trees and fences in front of me and the stick being pulled back hard from the rear seat, taking us out of the fog and into the sunlit sky at quite a steep angle. Perhaps if I had cross-checked with the other instruments instead of concentrating on the artificial horizon I would have seen that the altimeter was showing a descent in spite of what I saw on the artificial horizon, the latter having, as I later found out, a considerable acceleration error, when it was possible to indicate a nose-up attitude although the aircraft was descending.

By now we were safely climbing and I thought that the excitement was over for the day. How wrong I was! We advised the airfield that fog was now at the edge of the runway, and expected a quick recall, but being No. 203 AFS, this could not be done without reference to a certain wing commander, and this took time. No decision had been made by the time we reached 30,000 ft, but we noted that the fog was now encroaching on the very end of the runway. Eventually we received the hoped-for decision: we were to return as soon as possible. With throttles closed and airbrakes out, Reg stood VW455/M on its nose and we hurtled earthwards, but only for a few thousand feet, as the brakes came in and the throttles were opened again. Reg had sinus trouble, and the sudden increase in pressure was giving him considerable pain. The fog now covered one-third of the runway, and aircraft could be seen landing on the clear bit. We tried another fast descent but it was no go – more pain apparently. Fog also covered most of the surrounding country, as well as half of the runway, and with our slow descent, half became nearly all, with one last aircraft sneaking in at the last moment.

We were now the only aircraft left airborne, and the decision was made to divert us to Carnaby, the emergency airfield with a longer and wider runway that was built during the Second World War to accept damaged aircraft returning from raids. The only snag was that Carnaby was also under fog, which was of the thin variety through which one could see directly down, but not obliquely. This enabled us to see the airfield below us, but not if we did a normal approach. Fuel was not critical at this stage but we knew that if we needed to fly for long at circuit height this would soon change. As soon as we left the airfield for even a close circuit it was lost to view, but it was worth trying, and as Carnaby had homing facilities we asked for a steer in the hope of being in a position to land. By this time we were down to treetop height, luckily over level ground, with wheels and flaps down, flying as slowly as possible and making any turns as gentle as possible so as not to induce a stall

Reg took us up to 1,000 ft for another look around, during which we received a call from Driffield that I didn't hear. He suggested another go, so it was down to the trees again and more steers, with Reg flying and my eyes out on stalks in the front. Suddenly, just off the right wing, a grey shape appeared. We were parallel to the runway but we didn't know how much of it was left. It was our last chance, so with a quick right turn, it was onto the runway at forty-five degrees. The landing was virtually a controlled crash, and we then taxied through the fog to the control tower, where we stopped engines, pulled the lever to open the long hood, breathed damp air and heaved great sighs of relief. Reg went off to phone Driffield while I wandered around the aeroplane. Several minutes later, he returned looking glum. Pete Rees, another trainee pilot, had gone in on take-off in VW448, which meant he had probably done as I had done and paid too much attention to the artificial horizon. However, he had no instructor with him as a second pair of eyes. [VW448 crashed near the village of Kirkburn, to the south west of Driffield, having hit obstructions shortly after take-off.] At Driffield we had barrack accommodation, and Pete's bed was opposite mine, which tended to make matters worse.

We waited for an hour or so for the fog to clear, by which time we had refuelled, and as soon as possible taxied out to the runway, being anxious to get back to base. After take-off the wheels were selected up but nothing happened; our arrival at Carnaby had obviously broken something, so with permanent three greens we set off back to Driffield, where, on inspection, a large crack was found in the undercarriage system. The whole fiasco made the local newspapers, with both Pete's accident and our adventure being mentioned. It was on the way back to Driffield that Reg told me about the radio message that I hadn't heard. The instruction was that if we didn't make it next time round, we were to point the aircraft out to sea and jump over the side, or however it was one left a Meteor. This had not gone down too well with Reg, whose parachute was overdue for repacking, and it had made him even more determined to get down if at all possible.

After serving in the Middle East, Bob Hillard became a ferry pilot, a job that entailed delivering a wide number of aircraft types, including many different variants of Meteor, throughout the UK:

I only once got my hands on an Meteor F.3 when I took EE340 from Oakington to Llandow, refuelling at Aston Down. One thing you had to watch on the F.3 was the brake pressure, as there was no engine compressor, so what you had when you started was what you had to land with. One of our chaps disappeared off the end of Llandow's runway because he hadn't read the Pilot's Notes. I did not find it particularly impressive, although I suppose it had already seen plenty of service. The F.4 was pleasant enough and was just like a single-seat T.7 as far as I was concerned, and certainly there were no untoward happenings with it. A version of the F.4 that I could have done without, however, was the U.15 target drone. I took VZ389 from Tarrant Rushton to Aston Down, and a right wreck of an aircraft it was – scruffy, and still in its old paint. To make matters worse I had to pump down the undercarriage when I got to Aston Down. Still, it was only going to be shot down at Llanbedr, I suppose. Thankfully it was my only U.15.

The T.7, of course, was always around to be ferried. We were also obliged to do periodic checks in them at the FTU at Benson. The only slight problem I had with a T.7 was when approaching Kirkbride, when the ASI stuck at 130. Luckily I was able to feel the sink in time to put on power, but it was a problem that, as far as I know, hadn't happened before. The jolt of landing was sufficient to make the ASI read correctly, but an inexperienced pilot could have been in trouble. The F.8 also turned up frequently with aircraft needing to be picked up from the MUs and delivered to the squadrons. I had no mishaps in them, and the same applied to the FR.9. I also flew the night-fighter Meteors, which were a pleasant bunch to fly, nice and steady, perfect for the A to B stuff that we used them for. I couldn't help thinking that they were just too stable to be good fighters, but I suppose that they would not have been thrown around the sky like normal day-fighters. The NF.14 had to be the best of the lot with that nice clear canopy, which was superb for formation flying. I notice from my logbook that I ferried NF.11 WD604 on 20 January 1953 from Bitteswell to Wroughton. This aircraft was rather unusual, as it was used to conduct trials with jettisonable wingtip tanks.

Before flying Venoms and Javelins with 89 Squadron in the night/all-weather role, Paul Hodgson flew Meteor day-fighters, and recalls his impressions of the aircraft:

My Air Force career on jets began in the early 1950s training on Meteor F.4s and T.7s at Full Sutton. I then flew F.8s on No.226 OCU at Stradishall, followed by three years with 64 Squadron at Duxford. My recollections of the F.4 are somewhat hazy, although I do remember that the Derwent 5 engines had a tendency to flame-out at altitude unless the throttles were moved very carefully, and that the relight buttons were impossible to reach without slackening one's harness. They were mounted on the front of the throttle panel. This was also a problem on early Mark 8s, but their engines were far less throttle sensitive. Later, modifications on the F.8 put the relights on the HP cocks.

The Meteor F.4 and the early F.8s were fairly heavy to fly at high Mach numbers with their gear-tab ailerons; later versions of the F.8 were fitted with spring-tabs, and these were a big improvement. Another problem was icing of windscreen and canopy, both at altitude and on descent, but once again this was greatly improved on later F.8s. The other developments

number of Meteors took part in engine trials, including WA820, which was re-engined with
mstrong Siddeley Sapphires. On 31 August 1951 it was flown by Flight Lieutenant Tom Prickett
attain a 'time to height' record, reaching 39,370 feet in 3 minutes 7 seconds. (*Philip Jarrett*)

eteor F.8 WA829 'A' of 245 Squadron. (*Philip Jarrett*)

A neat echelon port formation flown by Meteor F.8s of 56 Squadron. (*Philip Jarrett*)

Armstrong Whitworth-built Meteor NF.12 WS697 of 25 Squadron (*Philip Jarrett*)

Meteor F.8 VZ521 was the personal aircraft of Flight Lieutenant Joe Maddison of 74 Squadron. He is seen here taxiing at Horsham St Faith in the summer of 1952. (*Alan Colman*)

Pilots of 74 Squadron look suitably pleased as they show 'Miss Trinidad' the cockpit of a Meteor F.8 at Horsham St Faith in late 1953. (*Alan Colman*)

eteor A77-855 was flown in the Korean War by 77 Squadron of the RAAF. (*Philip Jarrett*)

A pair of Meteor F.8s of 245 Squadron on final approach to Horsham St Faith in January 1952. (*Alan Colman*)

A Meteor F.8 of 245 Squadron shows off its nose-mounted flight-refuelling probe. This unit was chosen to trial the new in-flight refuelling systems that were becoming available. (*Alan Colman*)

Two Meteor F.8s of 245 Squadron and an F.4 operated by Flight Refuelling Ltd take on fuel from a USAF B-29 tanker. By such methods six Meteors could be kept in the air for patrols lasting 24 hours. (*Philip Jarrett*)

Meteor F.8s of the Horsham St Faith Wing (74 and 245 Squadrons) fly over Grantham on 10 July 1952. (*Alan Colman*)

Three Meteor F.8s of 500 Squadron pull up into a loop. The lead aircraft (WF714) is painted in the distinctive colours of Squadron Leader Desmond de Villiers, with dark blue tail and white and green zigzag markings. (*Philip Jarrett*)

VW360 was the prototype for the Meteor FR.9 photo-reconnaissance aircraft that featured nose-mounted cameras. It was first flown on 23 March 1950 by Jan Zurakowski. (*via Author*)

The ultimate night-fighter variant of the Meteor was the NF.14. These are from 85 Squadron, which received its first NF.14 in May 1954. (*Philip Jarrett*)

Meteor T.7 WL475 of 211 FTS at Worksop in 1956. (*Alan Colman*)

Meteor F.8 WE936 of 211 FTS 'looking for trade' at 35,000 feet over the north Norfolk coast. Note the late-model clear canopy. (*Alan Colman*)

he Meteor NF.13 was a tropicalised version of the NF 11 for service abroad. This is WM321 of 19 Squadron, which was based in the Canal Zone in Egypt in 1953/4. (*Philip Jarrett*)

A total of 100 Meteor NF.14s were produced. WS782 of 85 Squadron displays its two-piece blown canopy and its long nose, which was further extended on the NF.14 to give a fuselage length of 51 feet 4 inches. (*Philip Jarrett*)

The Meteor has a long history of ejection seat trials with the Martin Baker company. Shown here is the first live runway ejection made by Squadron Leader J.S. Fifield at Chalgrove from WA634 on 3 September 1955. (*Philip Jarrett*)

Meteor FR.9 VZ603 flew with 2, 79, 208 and 8 Squadrons, in addition to the Fighter-reconnaissance Flight, before being struck off charge on 9 May 1960. (*Philip Jarrett*)

Instructors from 211 FTS at Worksop half-way through a formation barrel roll. The nearest aircraft is Meteor F.8 WK992. This photo was taken by Alan Colman through the canopy of a Meteor T.7. (*Alan Colman*)

Meteor FR.9 VZ602 displays the 'UU' code letters of 226 OCU *c.*1951. (*Philip Jarrett*)

RA491 was another Meteor allocated to engine testing. In its original F.4 form it was flown with Rolls-Royce Avon turbojets, but it is seen here after further modification, having been fitted with an F.8 front end and SNECMA Atar engines. (*Philip Jarrett*)

Camouflaged Meteor F.8s of 74 Squadron pull through the second half of a loop over the Norfolk countryside in the summer of 1956. (*Alan Colman*)

F.6 of 20 Squadron seen at Waterbeach during Exercise Stronghold in 1956. (Philip Jarrett)

Meteor T.7s of the Central Flying School aerobatic team in 1953. (*Philip Jarrett*)

Camouflage colours were reintroduced on Meteors *c.*1954, although prominent squadron markings were still to be seen. These are Meteor F.8s of 245 Squadron. (*Philip Jarrett*)

Many Meteors ended their days carrying out secondary duties, as typified by NF.11 WD767, which was converted to a TT.20 for drogue towing. (*Philip Jarrett*)

included bigger intakes and an improved hood. In its final form I found the 8 to be an excellent aircraft, easy to fly except at low speed on one engine. It had good visibility and nicely balanced controls, albeit with slightly mushy response, and was a stable instrument platform. At that time it was normally operated with a ventral tank, which didn't affect the handling but took the edge off the clean performance. It was occasionally used with underwing tanks for ferrying trips, and these did affect the performance considerably.

While I was with 64 Squadron we mainly operated in the air defence role, and most of our practice targets were other Meteors and USAF aircraft based in East Anglia. The F.8 in its final form was a match for the American F-80 and T-33, and could give a good run to the F-86 at low and medium levels. At altitude, however, it was no contest: the F-86 had no Mach problems and could simply dive away and then zoom back. The other aircraft that was occasionally encountered was the Canberra, which outperformed the Meteor in almost all respects and was usually found on exercises cruising at a height we could only dream of.

For training we used the Meteor T.7, which suffered from two particular problems. The first was the hood, which tended to open in flight, and was likely to make the aircraft uncontrollable unless it broke away, but if it did it was liable to hit the occupants as it departed. The other problem was what became known as the Phantom Dive. This could occur if the undercarriage was selected with the airbrakes out, since the wheels always came out slightly asymmetrically, setting up a yaw that could become uncontrollable. This caused a number of accidents where the aircraft dived into the ground on the downwind leg of the circuit for no apparent reason.

Like many hundreds of his contemporaries in the 1950s, Peter Vangucci trained on the Meteor T.7. He was subsequently to have a distinguished career in the RAF, one of the highlights being a tour as OC 19 (F) Squadron on Lightning F.2As at Gütersloh from 1972 to 1974. He eventually retired in 1984 with the rank of group captain, and here he recalls his introduction to jet-powered flight:

I found the Meteor to be very stable and easy to control when in formation, although a complete revision of engine-handling techniques was required. In the beginning the delayed response when making throttle adjustments was slightly troublesome, and the lack of a propeller to 'stop' the aircraft did cause a few problems. However, with practice, the new technique became much easier, and after a relatively short time one totally accepted the new jet-engine regime and thought nothing more of it. Of course the

121

leader in any formation was subject to the same slower engine response times, so relative movements were, in effect, no different from before.

The stall was straightforward, and, with one exception, so was the spin. The exception was stalling from a stall turn. Here, once the nose had translated some 30 degrees left or right from the vertical, full pro-spin controls were applied. Usually the aircraft auto-rotated while the nose dropped to a vertically down attitude (incipient spin stage), at which point the aircraft entered the spin proper. Occasionally, when rotating, the aircraft would try to enter a spin in the opposite direction to the applied controls. This hesitation could last for some time and could be a little disconcerting.

During normal single-engined handling the rudder-control forces until touch-down were, I found, quite acceptable, as most could be trimmed out. Rudder-pedal forces when establishing one's personal critical speed were high and tiring, but this was an academic exercise not used in a real emergency. The one dangerous situation was stalling the fin and rudder. This could be encountered by applying bank (normally only up to 5 degrees) to reduce rudder load to such an exaggerated extent that the rudder stalled. At this point the aircraft's nose dropped violently and yawed in the direction of the dead engine. We practised this at 10,000 ft because recovery was often not made until the loss of some 6,000 ft, but we had to stop demonstrating this phenomenon when we discovered that we were putting wrinkles in the rear fuselage.

I also got to fly the Meteor F.3, which was extremely heavy on the controls. Indeed, if you applied more than 30 degrees of bank you needed two hands to level the wings, even at quite low speed. The spring-tabs later made the control loads much more acceptable throughout the speed range. The highest I ever got in a Meteor was about 40,000 ft in an unpressurised T.7, which was very cold. Flights to such heights could lead to a mild dose of the bends after a while! For its time, and prior to the advent of swept wings, the Meteor was a good aircraft, albeit somewhat basic. Unfortunately it acquired a rather undeserved reputation for asymmetric problems, although the early high loss rates were probably due to inadequate instruction in the transition from piston-engined to jet-engined aircraft capable of much higher speed, but of much shorter endurance.

Bruce Spurr, a former QFI at No. 207 AFS and CFS, rates the Meteor as his favourite aircraft of all time, although he soon appreciated that it was liable to bite if mishandled:

The foot loads on the rudder when doing asymmetric overshoots were similar to a Mosquito. However, the Meteor had a greater amount of power available, and from the recommended decision height of 400 ft and 140 knots one could go round again on one with no loss of height. A Mosquito under the same conditions would require most of the height to be converted into speed while the aircraft was being 'cleaned up' and the single-engine climb speed of 160–165 knots achieved. The loss of an engine in normal flight posed no problem for either aircraft, and both were capable of aerobatics in the rolling plane on one engine. The problems came when joining the circuit, particularly attempting single-engine overshoots, which in the early 1950s were practised by both qualified pilots and students with an engine flamed-out or feathered. After losing somewhat in excess of seventy pilots in a very short time practising asymmetric circuits, the Air Force finally prohibited flaming-out Meteor engines below 3,000 ft, any single-engine work below that height being done with an engine throttled back (in this time there were only three genuine Derwent engine failures).

The so called Phantom Dive occurred if one allowed the aircraft to yaw excessively. When the undercarriage was selected 'Down', a hydraulic resistor in the starboard leg caused it to lower after the port leg to avoid a sudden surge in hydraulic pressure. This caused yaw, which the pilot had to correct until the mainwheels were fully extended. With excessive yaw, the fuselage and engine nacelles presented at an angle to the airflow caused turbulence and sudden loss of tailplane lift, a situation that was aggravated if the airbrakes were left out in the circuit. In addition, the long nose of the Meteor required an adequate area of fin and rudder, and its effectiveness was probably affected by the turbulent wake from the front fuselage. Thus the aircraft could suddenly be heading earthwards in a sideways dive, needing more height than was available for recovery. Even before this phenomenon was well known I had discovered that at virtually all cruising speeds the application of an excessive amount of rudder would cause a sudden nose-down pitch, sometimes almost giving negative 'g'. I always made my students do this once, and the violence of it caused them never to forget to keep the slip needle central.

The Meteor's good qualities, however, far outweighed the bad. On my first sortie I was flying it more precisely than the Mosquito on which I was quite experienced. It had the typical solid 'Gloster' feel, and there was no backlash in the controls. I always considered the Meteor to be an excellent gun platform, and most snaking was pilot induced, probably as a result of using the rudder to bring the gunsight 'pipper' onto the target. It was better to use aileron to give the required amount of turn to achieve accuracy of aim. I had very rare experiences of aircraft starting mild 'Dutch Rolling', which became worse if one tried to correct it. The remedy appeared to be to ignore it, change speed or do a turn. The cause was obscure but was probably due to a change in the centre of gravity as fuel was burnt.

Fuel consumption was always a problem on the early jets and the Meteor was no exception. The short endurance meant that to get a satisfactory amount of exercises completed one had to be active from the time the engines were started. It was standard practice to arrive back in the circuit with enough fuel to go round again if one was balked on the approach, i.e. about five minutes fuel, but it was not unknown for pilots to run out of fuel while taxiing back! One problem was that if ice formed on the windscreen after a rapid descent from height, one had insufficient fuel to wait for it to melt (many units provided a glycol-soaked rag in a small linen bag to wipe off the ice). In the whole of my flying career on Meteors the duration of each sortie averaged out at forty-five minutes. Of course, such close safety margins would not be tolerated today.

The incidents I experienced on Meteors were few and far between. On one occasion a student allowed the airspeed to fall 10 knots too low on a flapless approach. We were high on the glide path so a simple push forward on the stick would have put us right but at about 100 ft he chopped the throttles putting us in an irretrievable position. The resultant heavy landing broke the main undercarriage legs and the landing run was continued on the nosewheel and the ventral tank. A small fire in the ventral tank was rapidly put out by the crash tender and we both walked away from the scene. I also had an emergency in a Meteor F.4 immediately after take-off. I had rolled the aircraft intending to climb away inverted when there was a small explosion and the cockpit filled with smoke. I rapidly completed a circuit and as soon as I had stopped the engines I looked in the port engine nacelle. As I suspected, the oil tank filler cap was off and hanging on its captive chain, the smoke having come from oil burning in the compressor which also supplied warm air to the cockpit. On another occasion I was practising recovery from unusual attitudes "under the hood" in a Meteor T.7. My Safety Pilot toppled the gyro instruments by a few aerobatics, stood the aircraft on its tail as if doing a stall turn, closed the throttles and handed over to me as the aircraft did a tail slide. I duly recovered and pointed out to him (he hadn't noticed) that one engine had ceased to burn because of a reverse airflow through the engine!'

Check-rides quite often produced memorable sorties, as was the case for Trevor Egginton who, before becoming chief test pilot at Westland, flew Sabres with 67

Squadron at Wildenrath and Hunters with Nos 43 and 222 Squadrons at Leuchars:

'Most of my time on Meteors was either target towing for the squadron or instrument flying under the hood, although we tended to use the Vampire T.11 for this generally. Occasionally you got to fly the Meteor F.8 'deep breather' version with big intakes and a bit more power. It was a powerful beast and fun to fly, nicer than the T.7. The only lasting impression of the Meteor was my check-out with the famed Peter Bairsto [at the time a flight commander on 43 Squadron and later Air Marshal Sir Peter]. He made me fly to the absolute limit, below the normal safety speed on one engine low over the sea. On the final approach he failed one engine and cycled the airbrakes to exhaust the accumulator pressure so I had to pump down the undercarriage using the hand pump. The nose wheel took some effort to lock down against the slipstream. Then the flaps had to be pumped down.

When in the final stages prior to touch-down he unlocked the gear, leaving no option but to overshoot. With the maximum power that could be held on the live engine it would not climb with the gear and flaps down so it was back to the hand pump. The main gear took some effort to get up, believe me! I was eventually allowed to land. My right arm felt like jelly and I swear that one leg was six inches shorter than the other. It was a lesson I never forgot when flying multi-engined aircraft. The Meteor killed quite a few pilots over the years, mainly doing practice asymmetric flying, and the other killer, of course, was the Phantom Dive, when the pilot forgot to retract the airbrakes before lowering the gear. One of the pilots on my course at ETPS suffered this fate.

Ted Nieass was another member of 74 Squadron at Horsham St Faith in the early 1950s and later became a flight commander with 245 Squadron. He recalls his impressions of the Meteor:

The Meteor was a stable aircraft in formation, with good forward and sideways visibility from the cockpit. On initial introduction to jet aircraft there was a tendency for pilots to hunt with the throttle and airbrakes to retain position in formation because although there was plenty of power in hand to catch up, the momentum on throttling back required a fair amount of anticipation to avoid overshooting one's position since there was no propeller drag. With practice this could be nicely judged and close formation was pleasurable. Major Milholland, our USAF exchange C.O. on 74 Squadron, would take twelve aircraft on an aerobatic tailchase, an exercise in control to maintain position and avoid whiplash at the tail end.

Training exercises comprised circuits and landings, aerobatics, spinning, single-engine flying, practice interceptions, together with

Squadron and Wing battle formation practices where up to thirty-six aircraft would make a stream take-off and subsequent stream landing. We also carried out night flying in the local area, cross country navigation exercises at high and low level and took part in Sector and Group exercises plus Rat and Terrier interception exercises at 250 ft which were exciting. In addition all pilots were required to undertake practice instrument flying in the Meteor T.7 and to submit to annual instrument rating tests conducted by a squadron Instrument Rating Examiner. Cine gun and live air-to-air firing exercises were carried out regularly and once a year the squadron visited the Armament Practice Station at RAF Acklington for a two week intense period of air-to-air firing. Additionally, once every six weeks or so the squadron took over responsibility to maintain readiness in what was known as Exercise Fabulous, with armed aircraft on standby from dawn to dusk for a week, ready to intercept any incursion into UK airspace by the enemy to the East.

We had occasional scrambles to intercept unidentified aircraft approaching UK airspace but never encountered a potential enemy. Very occasionally we would detach to an airfield in RAF Germany for an overnight stop, being intercepted on the way out and back. We frequently met other Meteors on exercise, including Dutch and Belgian squadrons. Meteor versus Meteor combat was interesting and success in dogfights depended on the skill of the pilots. When we mixed it with RCAF Sabres however, it was a different matter. We could not match them for speed, although we could out-turn them at heights below 20,000 ft. We also intercepted Lincolns and USAF B-29s when the practice was to make steep diving attacks from a 90 degree overhead approach to try to nullify their armament. The most humiliating experience was trying to intercept John Cunningham in the Comet when he was doing the flight trials – we couldn't get near it!

During my time on Meteors in-flight emergencies were rare, at least in my squadrons, although there were one or two mid-air collisions. Engine failures were virtually unknown, although on one occasion I had one run down to a stop on me on the final approach to land. I was grateful that my normal practice as a leader of four, was to make a very steep approach, having made a break into a continual tight turn, climbing from 500 ft to circuit height of 1,000 ft. This kept my circuit tight and allowed the other three in the formation also to fly a tight circuit. In this instance had I been making a shallow approach the loss of an engine would have posed considerable difficulty in making the runway. On examination nothing was found to be wrong with the engine. While on the Day Fighter Leaders Course at West Raynham, a main undercarriage leg failed to lower which necessitated a landing on one main wheel and the nosewheel. This posed no real problem, I was able to keep the aircraft straight until flying speed decayed and I then gracefully executed a curve off the runway on two wheels and an engine nacelle. Damage to the aircraft was minimal, although I wrecked the boundary fence by jettisoning the ventral tank on the final approach at about 50 ft. Thinking back, this was a little fortuitous as it could easily have bounced and hit the aircraft. Finally, on an air-to-ground firing exercise my canopy parted company with the airframe. This caused no real difficulty since the Meteor F.8 was cleared to fly with the hood open, but the noise was deafening. It resulted with my aircraft being fitted with one of the first completely clear Perspex canopies which were starting to replace those with a metal rear end which degraded rearward vision.

All in all the Meteor F.8 was a pleasant aircraft to fly but it was rapidly being overtaken by the developments in swept wing fighters of which the F-86 Sabre was the first example. After 1950 it is doubtful if the Meteor could have coped as an interceptor fighter against the type of opposition which was developing behind the Iron Curtain. It was a sturdy and reliable aircraft with a good serviceability record, but was short in range and lacking a real all-weather capability. The Meteor F.4, which was relegated to training units by 1950, was rather more sluggish than the F.8 and, of course, had no ejector seat, a major concern for pilots since manual escape was difficult even in ideal conditions and virtually impossible if out of control. The T.7 again had no ejector seat, was unpressurised and cold at height, not as agile as the F.8 and was subject to one or two nasty accidents when the large canopy, hinged on the starboard side, became unlocked in flight, pivoted on its centre axis and effectively decapitated the crew. It was always a consideration when flying the T.7 to ensure that the canopy was properly locked.

Although engine failures were extremely rare, a certain law dictated that they were likely to occur at the most inappropriate moments as Peter Sawyer discovered

After learning to fly in Southern Rhodesia, I returned to the UK to convert to the Meteor at Driffield in 1949. The Meteor T.7 provided me with an everlasting memory. It was famous (or infamous) for its nasty habit of crashing when doing single-engine flying at too low an airspeed. I learnt early having an engine failure on take-off on my very first solo. I only realised this after an age when I found out why the beast was flying sideways. I remembered that I had to maintain speed on landing so I landed 40 knots too fast but managed to stop before running out of runway! It was a good start to jet flying but I never had another engine failure in a Meteor.

I did a tour with 1 Squadron at RAF Tangmere and what a wonderful time it was – a marvellous station and squadron. Memories are of "finger four" high level battle formation sorties involving practice interceptions of bomber aircraft or other squadrons, either Meteors or Vampires. It was good fun in a very pleasant aircraft with few vices. Other memories include formation aerobatics and the occasionally frightening Battle of Britain flypasts over London involving massive numbers of aircraft. I recall one such rehearsal when our formation of thirty-six aircraft met a similar sized gaggle of USAF F-84s at 1,000 ft over Southend Pier, head on. We all missed each other by some miracle and broke formation downwards to return to out various bases.

Like many British-built aircraft, the Meteor was if anything over-engineered and its basic strength resulted in many pilots surviving potentially fatal accidents. Derek Morter, who later led the Blue Herons aerobatic team on Hunters, was one pilot who owed his life to George Carter's design philosophy:

My Meteor training took place at No. 205 AFS, Middleton St George on F.4s and T.7s. On high level navigation trips we were given a glycol soaked sponge and a very basic home made dinghy knife made from a bit of hacksaw blade with a wooden handle. Descending from high altitude and very low temperatures we soon realised what the sponge was needed for as the front screens iced up completely. The knife was because a dinghy pack had blown up inadvertently in a Meteor T.7 (not at Middleton) forcing the stick forward with obvious consequences. Eventually we were all issued with a proper knife, but I never heard of anyone else having a dinghy blow up. The water however in the dinghy packs froze so one's rear suffered on many an occasion. I was grateful to be at Middleton St George where the casualties from single-engined circuits were far less than at Driffield. My first tour was with 74 Squadron – they were really happy days … Rat and Terrier exercises, Saturday morning balbos, combined service exercises. I was also an Instrument Rating Examiner (IRE) which meant that virtually all my flights in the T.7 were up to 30,000 ft and, of course, it was unpressurised. Despite this everyone lived!

One particular trip with 74 Squadron stands out in my memory. It took place on 26 August 1953 and I was flying VZ557, leading four aircraft on an early morning attack sortie in the Thetford Battle Training Area. The enemy was a Welsh Infantry Brigade, Territorial Army. On one pass several gesticulating Brown Jobs sheltering under a tree caught my attention. Their gestures did not seem complimentary to the Royal Air Force so I decided that they would be my next target. Suffice to say that I was so determined to teach them some manners that I left my pull-up a little late. I, and the Meteor, passed noisily through the upper half of several trees. I returned to base noting that the wing leading edges were very badly dented, the ventral tank had obviously been damaged because of its position, but both engines were running fine. I orbited base and watched senior officers' cars rushing to ATC as I burnt off fuel. I carried out a slow speed check, operated all the services and contemplated my now definitely uncertain RAF career. A successful landing was made after crossing the hedge 15 knots faster than normal.

The damage was severe, more extensive than I thought, and was assessed as Category 4 (Cat 5 was a write off!). The engines had swallowed so many leaves it looked as if someone had thrown gallons of green paint into the intakes. An inquiry was convened. In the meantime the Welsh invited me and the other three pilots to a dining-in night in order to "court marshal" me. The prosecution presented as evidence several relieved officers, many tree branches and soiled underwear. I hadn't a leg to stand on. From the RAF I earned myself an AOC's reproof and a lesson that I never forgot, but with untold gratitude and admiration for the strength of the "Meatbox" and its Rolls-Royce engines.

CHAPTER 15

Pilot Debrief (2)

Although the Meteor night-fighter did at least show a marked improvement in performance over the Mosquito NF.36/38 that it replaced, in terms of handling it was somewhat ponderous, and as the early variants possessed the same AI.10 radar as the Mosquito, there was no improvement in radar capability. Despite this, many pilots have fond memories of the aircraft, and although it was a long way from being a true all-weather fighter, its basic docility inspired confidence, especially for crews faced with an instrument letdown in bad weather at night. Howard Fitzer flew nearly 500 hours in Meteor NF.11s with 68 Squadron, followed by a further 264 hours on the NF.12/14 with 46 Squadron:

> Compared to the Vampire and Venom, the Meteor was stable, easy to fly and very popular, especially the NF.14 with its bubble canopy. Unlike some of the single-seat Meteors, I do not recall any directional snaking problems with the night-fighter version of the Meteor. Although it was a stable flying platform, it suffered from two salient problems typical of wing-mounted gun installations. The first was wing twisting, the severity of which varied with 'g' loading. This of course altered gun alignment, with consequent sighting inaccuracy. The second concerned 'harmonisation', or the gun alignment that determined the range at which the trajectories of all four guns converged. For the Meteor NF this was set at 400 yards, at which range gun-pattern density (concentration of fire) was therefore at its greatest. It follows that at lesser or greater ranges than 400 yards (i.e. before and after trajectory convergence) there was a consequent scatter effect, particularly at greater ranges.
>
> There are those who would argue that the resultant wider scatter of shot, despite loss of concentrated fire, would be a decided advantage in the NF role. Others would argue that the usual additional commitment to a day-fighter role would put the Meteor NF at a disadvantage in a combat environment that implied high 'g' loadings and difficulty in bringing to bear concentrated fire at a precise range. Although parallel fuselage-mounted guns typical of day-fighters also suffered a degree of pattern spread with

increasing range, it was considerably less than wing-mounted installations, thus permitting higher concentration of fire at virtually any range. Results tend to speak for themselves, as was apparent from the air firing results I obtained with the Meteor F.8 (fuselage-mounted guns) while attending the PAI Course at RAF Leconfield. My average air-to-air firing scores were consistently higher (up to ten times higher) than those I ever obtained in the NF versions – a fact that tends to highlight the airframe/harmonisation problems inherent in wing-mounted gun installations.

On an operational squadron, displaced head-on attacks at or above target level were the usual method of interception, mainly because potential targets had broadly similar performance and long tail chases, therefore, were usually impracticable. The use of 'window' or chaff by target bombers posed quite a problem, although in some instances it could be utilised as an indication of target position. In most cases it seemed to simply swamp the radar. The main problem for the pilot was to obtain visual sighting of the target at night, at that time a prerequisite to engagement with guns, the worst condition being a clear night without cloud or moon and over the sea, with no light source or background, and nothing to reflect it.

The highest I ever got up to was around 41,000 ft (after a very long climb). Flying the Meteor NF at that altitude was rather like trying to balance a plate on the point of a needle, and the slightest turn induced a loss of altitude. I felt that interceptions would have been near impossible. On one occasion I was chasing a Canberra at night during a NATO exercise. At approximately 36,000 ft, every time the aircraft reached Mach 0.78 the port wing dropped quite violently, making directional control very difficult. After a futile eighty-mile chase I was forced to abandon the interception and return to base due to shortage of fuel.

Among the hazards we faced were heavy bombers trailing aerials and any that were piston engined. The low speed of the target meant that a fighter could be caught in the slipstream and thrown about at speeds perilously close to the stall. This was a particular hazard to those squadrons that had a night 'anti-minelayer' commitment. Mine-laying aircraft typically flew at heights below 500 ft above sea level and at very low speeds, and since it was necessary to approach the target from below to avoid swamping the radar with sea returns, the task was sufficiently dangerous as to cause the loss of a number of aircraft. One other rather unpleasant habit was for some targets, usually Lincolns, to install microphones in their engines and tune in to interceptor frequencies – a delightful noise at full power!

I particularly remember the sequel to a NATO night exercise carried out during the 1950s. NATO had gathered together sufficient aircraft to launch a simulated '1,000-bomber raid' against the UK. At the appropriate time a number of UK-based night-fighter squadrons were launched to intercept them head-on, all participants being instructed to operate with navigation lights switched off in the interests of realism. The obvious problem did not unduly concern us since we were equipped with radar. At the end of the exercise all participants were instructed to switch on their navigation lights prior to returning to base, at which point the sky seemed to be lit up like a Christmas tree. I've never seen so many aircraft at night in my life – it was quite a sight!

Malcolm de Garis flew Meteor NF.11s with 29 and 125 Squadrons at Tangmere and Stradishall respectively, before converting onto the Venom NF.3. He gives his personal view of the Meteor as a night-fighter:

Although I always felt safe in the Meteor and still have a strong affection for the aircraft, it was never an effective interceptor as the opposition was generally higher and faster, and the average maximum range of the AI.10 radar was only around ten miles where a minimum of twenty miles was required. The aircraft handled reasonably well at 40,000–42,000 ft, but the engines were hard pushed and were only good for 200 hours before overhaul. I was lucky to serve on units that expected one to handle the engines in accordance with best practice. I only ever had one Derwent failure, and that was when I spent a short time on a training unit that, surprisingly, did not conform to this rule, as was obvious from the rude noises emanating from taxiing aircraft. The ailerons on the NF.11 were heavy at 'high' speed, otherwise control loads were considered good at the time. On the two squadrons I served with it was rare not to have wing tanks fitted, consequently speeds were never very high.

A lot of our time was taken up with practice interceptions and cine gun practices under GCI control. Once contact *Judy* had been called, the target would weave and, at night, switch off his navigation lights. The GCI would be asked to vary the initial interceptions anywhere between ninety degrees to head-on if the aircraft radar was up to it. A successful interception would end with a cine gun attack (day only). During exercises anything and everything could, and did, happen, which was very realistic and of far more value in terms of training. One thing we did on 29 Squadron was low-level anti-minelayer interception practice. Radar range was pathetic but was helped by the comparatively low speeds flown. One had to be careful not to lose height in turns as it could spoil one's day and dreadfully upset 'you know who' in the back. We were fitted with a jamming homer called 'Appendix' attached to one of our two VHF radios, enabling us to practise anti-jamming intercepts, but that only applied to major exercises.

I did not have any big problems on Meteors, although two incidents got the adrenalin going at the time. The first was at night when we had a fire in the back cockpit a long way from home. Once on the ground, it was discovered to be a burnt-out radar control unit; you only have to read the various books now available on wartime night-fighting to see how common an occurrence that was. The second was also at night, when the aircraft started shaking and banging. As luck would have it our 'playmate' was the boss, and in reply to my shaking voice, he gave a reassuring opinion that it was a fluttering Westland valve. He was right, as bosses usually are!

Like many other pilots, one of Barry Holmes's most vivid recollections of the Meteor was the asymmetric training that he had to endure at 205 AFS at Middleton St George. After operational training at 228 OCU, Leeming, he went on to fly over 700 hours on NF.11s with 68 Squadron at Wahn as part of 2ATAF:

The Meteor T.7 was a bit of a handful. It required the full strength of one leg to hold the asymmetric thrust at high power, low speed; if you didn't lock your knee you experienced the original 'knee trembler'! Quite a few students were killed practising asymmetric (which we were allowed to do solo), including one at Middleton St George who went off the runway and crashed into the officers' mess, now the St George Hotel, Teesside Airport. His ghost is still reputed to haunt the place. Once you got to know it, however, and once the standard of asymmetric teaching improved, it presented no real problem. The secret, of course, was to avoid as much as possible the high power/low speed situation, and especially the long drag in on finals. It was much easier to rejoin on one engine by doing a standard fighter-type run-in and break. The Marks 4 and 7 were the worse for asymmetric. The Mark 8 was easier with the different fin and rudder, and the NF easier again with its increased fuselage length.

The normal type of interception we practised was the ninety-degree profile with, ideally, the target crossing about a mile ahead, or less at low level. The difficulty was created by the limitations of the AI.10 radar (of 1943/4 vintage) fitted to the NF.11. On a very good day this might have a range of some four miles, but more often was only two miles. Moreover, the antenna rotated through 360 degrees and was not stabilised; its coverage in elevation relative to the aircraft was controlled by the navigator using 'tilt' switches that controlled the upper and lower limits of its elevation scan. So every time the aircraft banked, the 'tilts' had to be used to hold the target in scan. This called for very good co-ordination between pilot and navigator, especially when trying to follow an evading target. Nevertheless, good crews achieved excellent results, even on some of the more esoteric exercises, such as night low level (at 250 feet) or night intruder, when we would intercept targets in the airfield circuit.

Almost all our practice interceptions were against other Meteor NFs. The normal procedure was to take off as a pair; then, alternately, one would act as fighter, the other as target, under the direction of a GCI. Only during exercises were we likely to meet other types of target; at night these were most likely to be Canberras. These were extremely difficult to get a 'kill' on at 40,000 ft; I recall following one for 150 miles about 1,000 yards behind, unable to close to gun range. I would put the nose down to pick up speed, get within range, pull back up to get to a firing position and just drop back to 1,000 yards again!

There was virtually no difference in aircraft performance between the different marks of NF. The Mark 14 was certainly the nicest to fly, mainly because of its all-Perspex canopy, which, apart from improving the view, gave more headroom. In the NF.11 you were always banging your head against the canopy structure. I cannot speak with authority about the radar performance of the NF.12/14; they were equipped with the AI.21 [British designation for the American Westinghouse APS-57]. This had a greater range capability, but it had a PPI scope instead of the 'B' scope of the AI.10, and this must have made target evasion more difficult to follow, especially at short range.

The Derwents in the later marks of Meteor had the improved burners, and we never had any surge/flame-out problems at high altitude – unlike the F.4, where you had to be very careful with the throttle at height. Indeed the Derwent was a most reliable engine, and I cannot recall anyone on the squadron having a genuine engine failure. I suppose that in today's era of fully powered controls, one would have to admit that the control forces were quite heavy at high speeds. The modification that added spring-tabs to the ailerons was a big improvement, and generally the controls were well balanced. On 68 Squadron we flew a four-aircraft aerobatic team called the Moonrakers. The evidence of the aerobatic team photos, where speeds were in the range 200–400 knots, shows that the NF was easily handled, though heavier than the day-fighter version.

Generally, problems were few and far between. There was one occasion when taking off in an NF.14 when I found that the ASI would not function and the altimeter was reading backwards! After becoming airborne the navigator told me that his ASI and altimeter were missing. I got him to plug the open tubes with his chinagraph pencils, upon which the instruments all started working again. It was my fault – I had taken the wrong aircraft, one which was still being worked on! Incidents were bound to happen, of course, like the airman on the squadron next door, working in the cockpit of an armed-up aircraft, who managed to fire off several rounds into the ventral tank of an aircraft in front, causing an interesting fire; or like the time when my No. 2 on a formation take-off retracted his wheels too soon and came to a somewhat abrupt stop. The Meteor was a very pleasant and easy aircraft to fly. It was difficult to get the best out of it as an operational night-fighter, when it could be frustrating from a radar and aircraft performance point of view, but I look back on it with a great deal of affection.

Despite its role as a night-fighter, the long-nose Meteor could not be described as sophisticated in terms of its navigation equipment or approach aids, so if weather conditions were to deteriorate, or were not as forecast, a serious situation could quickly arise. Flg Off Graham Elliott, a ferry pilot with 147 Squadron, found himself in such a predicament when delivering a Meteor NF.13 from Istres to Luqa in Malta:

Like all British fighters of the time, WM363 was equipped only with basic necessities – no autopilot, no powered controls and no radio aids to navigation. On 25 May 1955 it contained myself in the pilot seat, with navigator Flt Sgt Roy Bradley sitting behind me. We were flying at 35,000 ft over the southern end of Sardinia *en route* from Istres, in the south of France, to Malta. Our callsign was RAFAIR MGTWF, or Whiskey Foxtrot for short.

Earlier in the day, we had visited the met office to get the Malta weather, current and forecast. The cloud base was reported as 300 ft at Luqa. This was not unusual. Early-morning low cloud in the Mediterranean, and the forecast for it to burn off by lunchtime, with just scattered cloud at 2,000 ft and no cloud above that, was quite common. All in all, a fine summer day for the small island in a blue sea. Being a weather-conscious type, and in the knowledge that there was no alternative within range, I climbed the stairs to the met office every hour to check the latest weather at Luqa. The French civilian Met officer became increasingly irritated by this young Englishmen, speaking terrible French, who was interrupting his morning of smoking and magazine reading. It was my fault that he had to get up, go into the next room, and find the weather reports on teletype. These reports showed no improvement. Then, at 3 o'clock in the afternoon, he met me as I climbed the stairs and thrust a piece of paper into my hand. On it was written the latest Luqa weather – scattered cloud at 1,000 ft, thin scattered cloud at 7,000 ft, visibility ten nautical miles – exactly as forecast and expected. '*Bien – allez*', he said, and went back upstairs, pleased to get rid of me.

My flight planning showed that we would have 160 gallons of fuel on arrival, more than enough for a leisurely circle of the island and a look at the ships in Valletta harbour. We climbed in the clear blue sky up to 35,000 ft. The aircraft was behaving perfectly except that in the back, Roy was fiddling around trying (unsuccessfully) to make the 'Rebecca' work. We got a couple of VHF radio bearings from 'Corso Fixer', located at Ajaccio on the French island of Corsica.

'We haven't got those forecast winds. We've lost four minutes on flight plan so far', said Roy.

Well, not to worry. Maybe we could do without the guided tour around Malta, if we were to lose more time. By the time we saw Sardinia, we were out of range of any radio station, but visually we were right on track. Our next contact would be Luqa. Then the sea became obscured by cloud, and layers soon came up to meet us, until we were skimming along the tops. We had now been flying for an hour and a half, and had about thirty-five minutes of fuel remaining.

'I estimate we are 100 miles out now, Skipper', said Roy.

'OK, I'll give them a call', I replied. 'Luqa Approach, this is Whiskey Foxtrot. Do you read?'

No reply. I repeated the call and eventually heard the voice of a man who had had nothing to do all day, because nobody had been flying.

'Whiskey Foxtrot, go ahead.'

'Estimating overhead in fifteen minutes, request weather.'

He sounded slightly surprised, as he had not received our flight plan.

'The last weather was cloud base 200 ft, visibility half a mile … but it's not quite as good as that now. We've been down all day.'

It was now 6 p.m.

'Roger, request GCA.'

'GCA is off the air. We can only offer you a QGH.'

No choice of course. So that short, bald b…..d of a Met officer at Istres had lied to me, or was 'completely incorrect', as I politely wrote at the time.

Now everyone concerned was suddenly wide awake and sitting up straight.

'Whiskey Fox descend now to 20,000 ft.'

Decisions were now to be made. We were late, so had less fuel than planned, and faced the strong possibility of more than one approach if we were to get in. To save fuel, I shut down the port engine, opened the fuel crossfeed and wound on the rudder trim with the awkward little wheel below my left elbow. Down we went, into the cloud. We passed overhead Luqa at 20,000 ft still in cloud – came down to 12,000 ft and turned back towards the island, still descending.

'Descend at your own discretion', the controller said.

'You bet I will', I thought.

'Maintain present heading. You are cleared to land – no other traffic – change to tower frequency.'

Luqa airfield is 300 ft above sea level. At 600 ft suddenly there was the sea beneath us and the rocky cliffs of Malta straight ahead. But our day was not yet over. Clinging to the cliff top and rolling across the island was a layer of fog! It looked rather like icing on top of a cake. Between it and the cloud from which we had just emerged, was a fuzzy gap. I had the wheels down and partial flap extended just in case I could see the runway. I also had a lot of speed, because to apply full power on one engine at landing speed in a Meteor would mean a very sudden ending to the flight.

Over the cliffs, I gently descended into the fog, and at about 100 ft above ground saw runway lights away on the left side. Power on – hold it straight – wheels up – leave the partial flap – up to 200 ft and into a kind of 'slot' between fog and cloud. No horizon to help me. Now for our last chance – a timed circuit. I turned left carefully and straightened out in the opposite direction. The tower said they had heard me go by and that they had told the man in the runway caravan to start firing flares vertically to indicate the end of the runway. Now to restart the engine. Press down on the button on top of the high-pressure cock (which was out of sight down on the left side), and – the engine starts! Offering a quick thank you to Rolls-Royce, I even upped the throttles, while frantically winding the little trim wheel. For heaven's sake, hold the heading and attitude. Still at 200 ft. Check the timing.

'Roy, if we don't get in this time, I will climb straight ahead and when I jettison the canopy, you will bale out. Got that?' A pause, then a resigned, 'Roger, Skipper.' Of course, we did not have ejector seats.

And then, up through the fog, ahead and to my left, the amber flares from the caravan. Watch the timing – turn accurately. Now – there's a flare

– wheels down – runway heading – and there's another flare straight ahead! Speed back – flaps down – hold 115 knots, and gently down into the fog layer. Don't fly into the caravan. Then suddenly, perhaps 75 ft below, a horizontal line of red lights flashes past under the aircraft and I see white runway lights – not to one side, but on each side of me! Throttles closed. We are on – keep it straight – roll to the end – turn right and stop.

'Well done Sir', from the back seat.

I did not reply. We had 60 gallons of fuel remaining, not enough for another try. A Land Rover came out to lead us in.

'Tower, give my thanks to the man in the caravan.'

I thought about this flight afterwards. We did not have a means of contacting Luqa from Istres; there was no RAF base there so we depended on weather reports. I had a 'Master Green' instrument rating, which meant that I could set my own limits, so no rules were broken. I was familiar with the terrain around Luqa. We had only a short-range VHF radio as a communication and homing aid. The Luqa tower controller had the idea of firing the flares, which almost certainly saved the day for us. Why were we successful in the end? It was a combination of good work by the approach and tower controllers and a wide-awake man in the caravan. But to be honest, it all boiled down to that old pilot's friend – LUCK!

What happened afterwards? Roy and I should have gone for a beer (or two), but he could not come to the officers' mess and neither of us had civilian clothes with us, so we could not leave camp. He did not fly with me again, but a year later he walked away from another Meteor night-fighter, which crashed in Holland. I doubt if he wanted to fly in them again!

APPENDIX

Meteor Structural Failures, 1946–53

Date	Mark	Serial	Unit	Location	Remarks
09/05/46	F.4	EE518	Makers	Defford	Broke up during high-speed pull-up, pilot killed
13/09/46	F.3	EE490	CGS	Leconfield	Disintegrated following an attempted roll following a high-speed dive, pilot killed
05/05/47	F.4	EE578	CFE	Nr Grantham	Broke up during interception exercise with Spitfires, pilot baled out uninjured
23/10/47	F.3	EE385	54 Sqn	Lübeck, Germany	Structural failure during aerobatic routine, pilot killed
13/07/49	FR.5	VT347	Makers	Moreton Valence	Failure of rear fuselage during high-speed dive, pilot killed
24/04/50	F.4	VW287	226 OCU	Newmarket	Both wings failed following high-speed dive out of cloud, pilot killed
29/06/50	T.7	WA668	CFS	Little Rissington	Broke up during pull-up from high-speed run over airfield, pilot baled out uninjured
30/10/50	T.7	WA673	CFS	Salperton, Glos	Dived steeply out of cloud and broke up, two crew members killed

Date	Mark	Serial	Unit	Location	Remarks
17/04/51	F.	VZ527	66 Sqn	Linton-on-Ouse	Disintegrated over the airfield after a fast shallow dive and roll, pilot killed
01/05/51	T.7	WF786	71 Sqn	Nr Osnabrück	Hood detached and aircraft broke up after crew baled out
20/06/51	F.8	WA877	66 Sqn	Nr Scarborough	Both wings failed during aerobatics, pilot killed
23/08/51	F.8	WA84	92 Sqn	Nr Catfoss	Broke up after pilot lost consciousness due to anoxia
10/09/51	F.8	VZ510	263 Sqn	Southend	Control lost in cloud and broke up after high-speed dive, pilot killed
07/12/5	F.4	VT339	226 OCU	Nr Stradishall	Disintegrated during high-speed run, pilot killed
04/01/52	F.3	EE332	1 Sqn	Nr Bassingbourne	Broke up during high-speed run at low level, pilot killed
24/04/52	T.7	WA665	205 AFS	Nr Middleton St George	Lost control in cloud and broke up in dive, two crew killed
17/06/52	FR.9	VZ583	208 Sqn	El Firdan, Canal Zone	Broke up during recovery from a loop, pilot ejected
24/06/52	F.3	EE414	206 AFS	Nr Oakington	Broke up in cloud during aerobatic sortie, pilot killed
17/11/52	NF.11	WD723	228 OCU	Over North Sea, off Sunderland	Descended through cloud after practice interceptions and broke up at low level, two crew killed
05/02/53	FR.9	VW368	208 Sqn	Gebel el Ma'aza, Egypt	Overstressed during high 'g' manoeuvre at altitude, pilot ejected

Date	Mark	Serial	Unit	Location	Remarks
13/04/53	F.8	WH347	CGS	Leconfield	Broke up after high-speed pull up, pilot killed
18/08/53	F.8	WE964	66 Sqn	Over North Sea, off Filey	Starboard wing failed during high-speed tail chase, pilot killed
04/09/53	F.8	WA778	66 Sqn	Butlins Holiday Camp, nr Filey speed	Disintegrated during pull-up from low-level, high-run, pilot killed
08/09/53	F.8	WA712	209 AFS	Nr Hullavington	Pilot probably inhaled fuel vapour and lost consciousness. Aircraft subsequently broke up
19/09/53	F.8	WA836	74 Sqn	Coningsby	Broke up during aerobatic display, pilot killed
19/09/53	F.8	WA927	56 Sqn	Wyton	Both wings failed during high-speed run as part of aerobatic display, pilot killed
02/10/53	F.8	WE856	19 Sqn	Wolstanton, Staffs	Broke up during aerobatic display near pilot's home, pilot killed

Glossary

A&AEE	Aeroplane and Armament Experimental Establishment
AFS	Advanced Flying School
AGL	Above Ground Level
AI	Airborne Interception (radar)
AOC	Air Officer Commanding
ASI	Air Speed Indicator
ASP	Aircraft Servicing Platform
ATAF	Allied Tactical Air Force
ATC	Air Traffic Control
Broadcast control	The general location of enemy formations was broadcast by voice when electronic jamming meant that it was impossible to direct fighters in the normal manner
CFE	Central Fighter Establishment
CFS	Central Flying School
CG	Centre of Gravity
CL	Lift Coefficient
CRD	Controller of Research and Development
Daunt guard	A guard in the engine intake, named after test pilot Michael Daunt, who was sucked into an intake on one occasion and was only saved by prompt action by the ground crew in holding onto him and the pilot in shutting down the engine
Diver	Codeword for V-1 flying bomb
DBR	Damaged Beyond Repair
DME	Distance Measuring Equipment
Dutch rolling	`A motion consisting of a combination of roll and yaw
EAS	Equivalent Air Speed
EFS	Empire Flying School
ETPS	Empire Test Pilots School
FAI	Fédération Aeronautique Internationale

FTS	Flying Training School
FTU	Ferry Training Unit
GCA	Ground Controlled Approach
GCI	Ground Controlled Interception
GGS	Gyro Gun Sight
HP	High Pressure (fuel cock)
IAS	Indicated Air Speed
ICAN	International Commission for Air Navigation
IFF	Identification Friend or Foe
IMN	Indicated Mach Number
IRE	Instrument Rating Examiner
JPT	Jet-pipe Temperature
kts	Knots
LP	Low Pressure (fuel cock)
MU	Maintenance Unit
NATO	North Atlantic Treaty Organisation
OCU	Operational Conversion Unit
PAI	Pilot Attack Instructor
PPI	Plan Position Indicator
PSP	Pierced Steel Planking
QFI	Qualified Flying Instructor
QGH	A ground-controlled letdown procedure
RAAF	Royal Australian Air Force
RAE	Royal Aircraft Establishment
Rat and Terrier	The 'Rat' was a low-flying 'enemy' intruder that was intercepted by a fighter aircraft, or 'Terrier'
Rebecca	An instrument that gave homing and range information
RCAF	Royal Canadian Air Force
RFS	Refresher Flying School
rpm	Revolutions per Minute
RT	Radio Telephony
SMC	Standard Mean Chord
Snake Climb	A method used by formations of two or more aircraft to penetrate cloud. Aircraft would be spaced at regular intervals and the leader would call course changes which would be followed by the other aircraft after an appropriate delay

SOC	Struck Off Charge
TAS	True Air Speed
TMN	True Mach Number
TRE	Telecommunications Research Establishment
USAAF	US Army Air Force
USAF	US Air Force
VG recorder	Records an aircraft's speed (V) and acceleration ('g')
VHF	Very High Frequency

Index

Almond, A.J. 62

Alwan, Lt 98

Amor, Geoff 14-5

Armitt, Sgt E.D. 41-2, 45

Atcherley, AVM R.L.R. 51

Atkin, Alan 89

Bairsto, F/L Peter 125

Baker, Kenneth 98

Baker, Joyce 98

Barry, F/L Dennis 8-9, 11-3

Bates, Sgt P.J. 84

Bazarnik, S/L K. 84-6

Beard, F/L Bertie 52

Bird-Wilson, W/C Harold 55- 6

Black, Sgt W.H. 97

Blight, F/O K.J. 41

Blow, F/L H. 93

Blyth, F/L C.I. 42

Bones, F/O K.B. 99

Boulton, P/O P.R. 66-7

Bradley, Sgt Roy 135-8

Bridge, P/O M.J. 87

Briggs, F/L St John 82

Brook, AVM W.A.D. 94-5

Brooks, PII J.A. 91

Brown, C.E. 86

Brown, SAC Frank 90

Brown, F/L Kenneth 89

Cannon, F/L V.B. 42

Carter, George 3-4, 30

Carter, P/O Nick 116

Cartmel, F/Sgt B. 13

Churchill, Winston 115

Clarke R.C. 86

Cole, Eric 60

Colebrook, Sgt M.E. 42

Colman, Alan 47-54, 100-8, 111-2

Constant, H. 3

Conway, S/L Gordon 94

Cooper, Mike F/O 11, 14

Cowper, Sgt L. 46

Cranston, Sgt I 45

Crosby-Warren, John 6

Cruickshank, P/O O. 46

Cunningham, John 126

Cuss, J.F. 62

Dabin, Victor 78

D'Arcy, P/O J.R. 87

Daunt, Michael 5-6

Davie, S/L Douglas 5

Dawson, F/L R.L. 42

Dean, F/O T.D. 10

Deeley, F/O R. 64

de Garis, Malcolm 132-3

Derwin, F/O P.J. 67

Dixon, F/L R.H.B. 88

Drummond, Sgt Vance 45

Dryland, Rodney 56, 62

Durrant, F/L A.M. 82

Eastman, F. 115-7

Egginton, Trevor 124-5

Elliott, F/O Graham 135-8

Evans, Sgt Derek 96

Evans, S/L Edgar 80

Fisher, F/L R.F. 90

Fitzer, Howard 130-2

Ford, P/O S.B. 81-2

Foster, Sgt K.H. 41

Foster, Sgt Mick 117

Fox-Linton, S/L Richard 76

Franklin, Eric 69

Frost, Charles 86

Furness, P/O G. 89

Galland, Major Adolf 56

Glover, P/O J.C. 77

Gogerly, F/O Bruce 45

Goorney, F/O A.B. 84

Goulding, John 60

Greensmith, F/O P.G. 64

Gregg, F/Sgt Donald 13

Griffith, A.A. 3

Guthrie, W/O R.D. 41-2

Hale, Sgt George 46

Halford, Frank 5

Hart, F/L W.I. 86

Hill, F/L G.W. 86

Hillard, Sgt Bob 96, 117-120

Hives, Ernest W. 5

Hodgson, Paul 120-1

Holland, F/O J.W. 79

Holmes, Barry 133-5

Hopkins, P/O D.G. 77

Hubble W/C John 46

Hulse, F/L Graham 57-8

Irlam, Sgt Dave 46

Jenkins, P/O R.W. 91

Jenkins, F/O S.T. 77

Johns, Gordon 88

Johnson, Maj Gen Leon W. 45

Jones, AM George 44

Kniveton-Thorpe, R.J. 60

Lett, J.H. 63

Lockyer, F/L A.D. 61

Maddison, F/L Joe 47

Martin, Sgt J.A. 60

Martin, W.D. 91

McDowall, S/L Andy 10

McKernan, P/O A.A. 98

McNair, P/O M.J. 92

McKenzie, F/O 11

Mead, F/L R.G. 76

Middlemiss, F/Sgt W. 45

Michelson, W/O W.S. 42

Milholland, Major G.W. 47, 125

Miller, S/L John 88

Millikin, F/O Lionel 60

Moffat, P/O D.H. 77

Morris, Bertram 84

Morter, F/O Derek 49, 128-9

Moss, Llewellyn 55

Myers, Sgt E.J. 42

Napier, Gus 49

Nieass, Ted 125-7

Norman, F/O Raymond 78-9

O'Shaughnessy, Sgt P.W. 97

Panton, Sgt I.H. 94

Poppe, P/O P.J. 62-3

Ralph, F/L F.A.O. 79

Rees, F/L 46

Rees, Pete 119

Rhodes, PII D.J. 91

Sanderson, S/L T.D. 79-80

Sawyer, Peter 127-8

Sayer, P.E.G. 4

Schnitzler, Sgt B.D. 59

Shanahan, SAC P.K. 84

Sharp, Denis 97-9

Simmonds, P/O Bill 46

Slessor, ACM Sir John 44

Smallwood, W/C D.G. 87

Spurr, Bruce 111, 115, 122-4

Stacey, F/L Peter 83

Steege, W/C Gordon 43-4

Stewart, Sgt S.J. 94

Stonham, Pete 107

Surman, P/O J. 46

Susans, W/C Ron 45

Taylor, F/O H.M. 79

Tomalin, W/C Charles 58-9,
    82

Thomas, F/L C.G. 41

Thompson, Sgt Bruce 45

Thompson, William 60

Thornton, F/O G. 41-2

Turner, F/L A. 99

Turner, P/O M.J. 81

Vangucci, Peter 121-2

Walz, P/O J.D. 95

Ward, F/O P.R. 66

Warwick, Sgt M.W. 65

Watson, H.R. 68

Watts, S/L L.W. 8, 13

Westcombe, Peter 87

Weyland, Lt Gen O.P. 45

Whatton, P/O B. 64

Whittle, Frank 3, 5

Willby, F/O W.F.B. 93

Williams, F/O H. 61

Willis, PII Reg 117-9

Wilson, S/L D.L. 41

Wilson, W/C H.J. 6, 8-9

Wilson, Ian 9-10, 13-4

Woodruffe, Sgt N.M. 41

Yule, W/C Bob 50